June Four

June Four

A Chronicle of the Chinese Democratic Uprising

by the photographers and reporters of the *Ming Pao News*

**translated by
Jin Jiang
and
Qin Zhou**

90-1532

The University of Arkansas Press

Fayetteville 1989 London

Originally published as *Bei Zhuang de Ming Yun* by Ming Pao Publishing House, Hong Kong, June 1989
93 92 91 90 89 5 4 3 2

DESIGNER: John Coghlan
TYPEFACE: Palatino
TYPESETTER: University of Arkansas Printing Services

The paper used in this publication meets the minimum requirements of the American National Standard for Permanence of Paper for Printed Library materials Z39.48-1984. (∞)

Library of Congress Cataloging-in-Publication Data

Pei chuang ti min yün.   English
      June Four: a chronicle of the Chinese democratic uprising/by the photographers and reporters of the Ming pao news; translated by Jin Jiang and Qin Zhou.
          p.   cm.
      Translation of: Pei chuang ti min yün.
      ISBN 1-55728-140-8 (alk. paper)
      1. China—History—Tiananmen Square Incident, 1989.   I. Jin Jiang
II. Qin Zhou   III. Ming pao.   IV. Title.
DS779.32.P4513   1989
951.05'8—dc20

                                                                          89-20260
                                                                          CIP

No publication bearing the imprint of The University of Arkansas Press has been acquired with more effort than the acquisition of this book has demanded or produced with so great a sense of urgency.

The importance of its publication lies not only in the fact that it is the first day-by-day record of the Chinese democratic uprising in book form, but also in the fact that the photographers and reporters of the newspaper *Ming Pao*, whose work it is, are Hong Kong citizens who could melt into the crowds at Tiananmen Square, taking pictures and asking questions without attracting great attention and being run off the streets as quickly as western journalists.

June Four is a diary, beginning and ending abruptly, as the uprising did.

Introduction

A pro-democracy movement triggered by the death of Hu Yaobang, the former general secretary of the Chinese Communist Party, recently swept mainland China, building up to mammoth demonstrations that were without precedent in the history of the People's Republic. The whole world was impressed by the peacefulness of the mass movement and by the restraint of the authorities for seven weeks; then troops opened fire on defenseless students and citizens and cleared the so-called "reactionaries" from Tiananmen Square.

The Chinese authorities proclaimed martial law in Beijing on May 20, but the students and citizens simply ignored it. Although this hurt the prestige of the government, in fifteen days the leaders again repeated that they would not use troops to deal with the students. Suddenly the army began a savage slaughter of demonstrators. Given a choice, we would rather have had martial law enforced thoroughly from the outset, so that the people at least would not have been so unaware of the coming massacre and been indiscriminately killed. The Chinese government employed typical Maoist practice and smashed the demonstration in one blow. Although the government cleared Tiananmen Square and reimposed order, the result was disastrous for the country and the people.

To the Chinese people at home and overseas as well, the massacre is a horrible lesson. Good will and reasonable hopes have been shattered; confidence in the government is gone. Pessimists may be resigned to the circumstances, while radicals, in desperation, risk arrest or go underground.

To foreign governments and investors, the irrational action of the Chinese leaders makes them suspicious as to whether this government can be trusted to protect their rights and interests in China.

The massacre will slow down China's modernization and put the living standard of Chinese people even further behind that of developed countries. Discontent will surely increase, and the government may disintegrate.

After the darkest night, we expect the light of morning, the dawn. But are we sure that what we have seen is the darkest?

This book collects more than two hundred photographs and covers every important event daily from Hu Yaobang's death to Deng Xiaoping's reappearance on television on June 9. The massive democratic movement showed the nation's yearning for freedom, human rights, "rule by law," and modernization. Our hope is that this book will help us and our children remember this terrible moment of sorrow in China's history.

The Ming Pao Publishing House
June 10, 1989

人民永不會忘記……

Wang Dan (holding megaphone).

Wuer Kaixi (center).

Student leaders: (from left) Feng Congde, Chai Ling, and Li Lu.

People Will Never Forget

More than three thousand hunger strikers were taken to the hospital.

A student cuts a stencil at the base of the Monument to the People's Heroes.

Young friends make copies of a leaflet.

For A Better Tomorrow

爲了更好的明天

The student broadcast station on Tiananmen Square.

Using a mimeograph, students work hard to get their information out.

Living conditions **are** bad, but the students hold out.

Bread and steamed buns are the students' main food for twenty days.

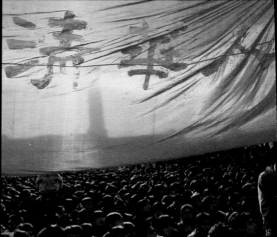

Workers demonstrate to support the students.

The Qinghua students are in action.

The general logistics department of the PLA supports the students.

Medical staff of Xiehe Hospital show their support for the students.

Personnel of the History Museum support the students.

Journalists of the People's Daily demonstrate for freedom of the press.

June 9, Deng Xiaoping shows up and approves the massacre.

Put down butcher's knife, become buddha now.

Older professors give support to their students.

The young people are hungry, but they are too concerned to eat.

Clothes from citizens warm the students.

Students sleep in camp on Tiananmen Square.

One person falls, hundreds and thousands of students go with him.

For a better tomorrow, I volunteer for the

Students on hunger strike.

We love the country, but does the country love us?

*You must study hard and carry on your big sisters'
and brothers' struggle.*

*After the International Children's Day, the blood
of big sisters and brothers will flood the ground here.*

Innocent children, will you remember the fourth of June?

June Four

April 15, Saturday
Hu Yaobang Dies

The former general secretary of the Chinese Communist Party (CCP), Hu Yaobang, dies of a heart attack.

It is rumored that the Central Committee of the CCP changed Hu Yaobang's obituary four times before finally releasing it. The obituary praises Hu as a "long-tested, loyal communist, a great proletarian revolutionary and statesman, an outstanding political commissar of our army, and a brilliant leader of the Party who, over a long period of time, served important Party positions."

Reviewing Hu's distinguished life, the obituary declares that "Comrade Hu Yaobang's death was a heavy loss for our Party and our people. He was devoted to the people and to the cause of Communism, served both with unstinting loyalty; he was moderate and eager to learn; he led a simple life, always placing the interests of the Party before his own needs. We shall learn from him and turn our sorrow into energy. Under the leadership of the Central Committee, we shall continue our cause in building Chinese socialism."

Hu Yaobang died of myocardial infarction, April 15, 1989, at the age of seventy-three.

April 16, Sunday

At midnight of April 15, a few hours after Hu's death, students on university campuses throughout Beijing began a spontaneous outpouring of eulogies, poems, and essays in Hu's memory, praising his accomplishments, complaining of the unfair way he was treated, and contrasting his honesty and integrity with widespread government corruption. One slogan on the campus of Beijing University (Beida) reads: "Anyone but Hu should have died"; another couplet says: "Mao is down, D is down, history will assign them places; Chou is gone, Hu is gone, they left with sad and anxious faces." D refers to Deng Xiaoping, and Chou is Chou Enlai. Chou and Hu are remembered as upright leaders who had the interests of the people at heart. Indeed, Chou's death in April of 1976 triggered a mass movement on Tiananmen Square, but this so-called April Fifth movement was put down by Mao and his followers.

People begin to stream into Tiananmen Square to mourn Hu's death. Under the Monument to the People's Heroes, pieces of white cloth and wreaths begin to accumulate. Some wreaths are signed; others are not. As the crowd of mourners grows larger and larger, the police arrive to keep order.

The Central Committee of the CCP decides to form a funeral committee for Hu, to allow his remains to lie in state in the Great Hall of the People so that citizens can pay their respects, and to fly the flags at half mast in Tiananmen Square, at Xinhuamen Gate, on provincial capitol buildings, and at all border crossings. It is also decided that Hu's memorial service will be held in the Great Hall of the People on April 22, and that the ceremony will be patterned after the funeral of Ye Jianying, the former president of state and key Party official. This is unusual since, unlike Ye, Hu was not a member of the Standing Council of the Central Committee at the time of his death—nor even in good standing with the Party since he had been forced by hard-liners to step down after the 1986–87 student demonstrations.

Students from Beida hold a sit-down protest on Tiananmen Square, demanding to attend the memorial meeting.

April 17, Monday

In the morning, the Central Committee invites some notable non–Party members to attend a forum in the Great Hall. At the suggestion of Zhao, who in January 1987 succeeded Hu as general secretary of the CCP after Hu was forced to step down, all those in attendance rise to their feet in silent tribute to the departed leader.

On Sunday evening, students from Beijing University (Beida) had sent eight wreaths in honor of Hu and placed them at

Seven demands raised by Beida students.

Off campus students parade the streets in memory of Hu Yaobang.

the Monument to the People's Heroes in Tiananmen Square, but the wreaths were removed during the night. The next day, about three thousand Beida students march twelve miles to the Square and deliver a petition to the Standing Committee of the People's Congress. The petition includes seven demands: to restore Hu's reputation as a servant of the people; to end the Party-sponsored campaigns of "opposing bourgeois democracy" and "cleaning up bour-

Many dazibao *(big character posters) appear on campus of Beijing Normal University.*

geois mental pollution" (The major cause for Hu's forced resignation was criticism of his loosening of Party control over ideological affairs.); to establish guarantees of freedom of speech and of the press; to increase the budget for education; to announce the right to peaceful public demonstration; and to end favoritism and corruption by high-ranking officials. In the afternoon, about five hundred students from China University of Political Science and Law march to the Square carrying a huge wreath; several hundred students stay on that night to guard this tribute to the fallen leader. In the meantime, rumors circulate that the Standing Committee of the People's Congress has turned down the students' petition.

There are also spontaneous activities and demonstrations in Hu's memory in Shanghai, where the Municipal Committee of the CCP announces limitations on activities. University students and citizens write poems and essays and put up posters both to mourn Hu's death and to call for democratic reforms.

April 18, Tuesday

About five thousand students from Beida, People's University, the University of Political Science and Law, Beijing Academy of Economics, and the Central Nationalities Institute march to Tiananmen Square, shouting "reject autocratic rule," "long live

Students mourn the upright official's death and oppose the corrupt officials. The banner says: "Social unrest results from corrupt bureaucrats."

democracy," and "clean up corruption," and begin a sit-in. Students from Qinghua University and other colleges also march to the Square for silent sit-down demonstrations in tribute to Hu's memory. By the afternoon, there are more than thirty thousand people in the Square, and police surveillance is noticeable.

At eleven o'clock that night, a thousand students try to send a wreath to the Xinhuamen Gate, one of the entrances to Zhongnanhai, the headquarters of the Central Committee of the CCP.

On the night of his return from Japan, Premier Li Peng goes to Hu Yaobang's residence to pay his respects. It is reported that when Li Peng saw Hu's widow Li Zhao, he broke into tears and asked if there were anything he could do for her. Hu's wife said that Hu had hoped that the Central Committee would give recognition to his work for the Party.

April 19, Wednesday
The First Conflict between Police and Students

The Xinhuamen Gate incident: At 12:20 A.M. more than one thousand students come to the Xinhuamen Gate and try to send a wreath and the petition into Zhongnanhai. The armed police form a wall of human bodies to stop the students. Meanwhile, more and more people gather outside the Xinhuamen Gate; eventually, some ten thousand people crowd to the gate and clash with police. One student is arrested, and a policeman is wounded by broken glass. A Hong Kong reporter is held by the police for a time and his film is exposed. At 4:20 A.M. officials broadcast warnings for everyone at the Xinhuamen Gate to disperse, and at about five o'clock order is restored.

During the day, university students keep marching to the Square, carrying huge portraits of Hu and slogans praising him as "the soul of China" and "democratic Yaobang." These are eventually placed at the Monument to the People's Heroes in the center of the Square. By eight o'clock in the evening, it is reported that more than one hundred thousand students and citizens have gathered there. Students sit on the ground, singing "The Internationale" and shouting "clean up corruption." That night the Monument becomes the stage upon which students and the teachers who have joined them speak on democracy.

At eight o'clock in the evening, Chen Xiping, Liu Yandong, and Sun Shixiong, deputies to the National People's Congress sent by the Municipal Party Committee, come to the door of the People's Great Hall and accept a petition including seven demands from students of Beida and the People's University.

The Central Committee announces a funeral office led by Qiao Shi and Hu Qili, both members of the CCP Standing Council. It is also announced that the memorial service will be held on April 22 in the main room of the Great Hall of the People and that Hu's remains will be sent to Ba Boshan Martyr's Cemetery for cremation.

In Shanghai: Three thousand students rally outside Fudan University calling for the solidarity of the people in the quest for democracy. The students have planned demonstrations in downtown Shanghai but are dissuaded by university authorities. Inside the school, however, *dazibao* (a Chinese term for the character poster) fill the campus, attacking government corruption and *guandao* (official speculation in business) and criticizing Deng Xiaoping for failing to carry out political reforms.

Student leaders tell the students to sit down to prevent the mob from attacking Xinhuamen, April 19.

April 20, Thursday

The second conflict at the Xinhuamen Gate: Before midnight, some twenty thousand people gather at Xinhuamen Gate. Reinforced by trucks and about two thousand personnel, the police officials warn the demonstrators to leave in twenty minutes. Then, at 2:30 in the morning, armed police attack the crowd with clubs, brass belt buckles, and steel-plated shoes; the demonstrators respond by hurling bottles. During the conflict, more than one hundred stu-

dents and four policemen are injured. Most of the crowd then disperse, but about three hundred students persist in a sit-down protest, shouting "love of country is not criminal" and "long live Democracy." After three o'clock, the police start to drag the students away; according to our reports at least two students are arrested. By five o'clock in the morning, order has again been restored.

Because the authorized student unions fail to provide leadership for the movement,

8

Beida students initiate the organization of a Solidarity Student Union in Beijing to advance the seven goals of the student movement as set out in the petition. The Preparatory Committee of Beida Solidarity Student Union has already been organized, with nine members headed by Din Xiaoping. The committee announced "A Letter to All Universities in Beijing," declaring that the activities in Hu's memory have developed into a democratic movement and putting forward seven guiding principles for the movement, the principles that were set out in the petitions. The solidarity letter states: "The past failure of student movements has made us realize that we would have no power if we did not form an organization including representatives from all colleges and from all levels of society. We therefore propose that each college send its deputies to help organize the college council of the Beijing democratic movement." The letter states that the Preparatory Committee will adopt collective leadership

The Monument to the People's Heroes becomes a stage for public speech.

9

and a representative voting system, and will employ peaceful methods, such as sit-down protests, demonstrations, boycott of classes, and hunger strikes. As already noted, the seven principles include: 1) to restore Hu Yaobang's tarnished reputation, to state the real reasons for his resignation in 1987, and to give Hu's funeral the highest rank; 2) to reject the two campaigns of "cleaning up bourgeois mental pollution" and "opposing bourgeois democracy"; 3) to explain how education has become "the most severe failure of the government" and who is responsible for this failure; 4) to affirm freedom of the press and allow unauthorized newspapers to exist; 5) to investigate and affix the responsibility for repressing student movements; 6) to open up to public scrutiny officials' salaries, total income, and taxes; and 7) to announce *guandao* criminal cases.

Beida students say that their organization had telegraphed more than one hundred colleges in big cities two days before to call for national pro-democracy action in memory of Hu and in opposition to autocratic

rule, and that many campuses have already agreed to participate.

It rains in Beijing on the designated morning; the students demonstrate in the afternoon. Then, as night comes, students begin to leave Tiananmen Square. Five thousand Beida students walk back to their campus in an orderly procession.

The New China News Agency publishes an editorial asserting that "Retaining Social Stability Is the Major Consideration for the Present." Claiming that someone shouted "down with the CCP" during the Xinhuamen Gate incident and that the students had wounded four policemen, the editorial warns people to cool down and to make a clear distinction between right and wrong. According to sources within the Agency, the author of the editorial was Zeng Jianhui, who was the deputy minister of CCP Propaganda Ministry and also deputy director of New China News Agency. These leaks also indicate that the essay was not sent to Mu Qing, the director of New China News Agency, for confirma-

The armed police beat the students with brass buckles, April 20, Xinhuamen.

tion before it was published; Mu Qing is said to be very upset by this development.

Student demonstration in Nanjing, the capital of Jiangsu province, and in some other cities: On Thursday night, about one thousand students march from Nanjing University to the provincial government carrying slogans and shouting "clean up *guandao*" and "down with the dictatorship." On the campus of Nanjing University, students break bottles to show their anger at Deng Xiaoping. Demonstrations also take place in Shanghai, Tianjin, Wuhan, and Hefei.

More than one hundred scientists speak out for democratic reform.

Students in Nanjing break xiao-ping *(small bottles) while students in Beijing hang* xiao-ping *(play on the name of Deng Xiaoping).*

April 21, Friday
The First Student Boycott of Classes

The unauthorized Beida Preparatory Committee of Solidarity Student Union has been accepted by the majority of students. To protest the April 20 Xinhuamen Gate incident, in which the police beat students and reporters, Beida students declare a class boycott next morning. Some students at Qinghua University, the University of Political Sciences and Law, Beijing Normal University, and several other universities respond to Beida students and start a boycott at their campuses.

Yan Jiaqi, a widely-respected scholar who speaks out against despotism.

Bao Zunxin, a well-known intellectual and a fighter for democracy.

Escalation of student movement: As the students march into the Square in the morning, many citizens are already gathered, paying their respects to Hu in silent tribute and discussing the student movement. By noon, about one hundred thousand people are on the Square, and they cheer to welcome each group as it enters. At the same time, about three or four thousand students are sitting on the steps of the Great Hall of the People to protest the Xinhuamen Gate incident, holding a banner that reads "protesting atrocity." At three o'clock in the afternoon, several thousand people try to dash into the building but are stopped by the military. Then a student parade from journalism departments marches into the Square, carrying a banner that reads "Journalism should tell the truth," to protest the false story about the April 20 Xinhuamen Gate incident from New China News Agency. People cheer them enthusiastically. As night falls on the Square, there are at least two hundred thousand gathered around (some reports say four hundred thousand), including students, workers, and peasants.

The base of the Monument becomes a stage for public speeches. Students and other citizens speak on democracy and the future of the country.

Initiated by the famous poet Beidao, who once led a signature drive demanding the release of political prisoner Wei Jingsheng, forty-seven intellectuals including Bao Zunxin, Yan Jaiqi, Yu Haochen, Li Zehou, and Dai Qin sign a petition and try to deliver it into Zhongnanhai, the headquarters of the CCP Central Committee. The petition requests that the Committee approve the democratic movement and get rid of corruption. The Committee refuses to accept the letter which is then delivered to the Standing Committee Office of the People's Congress.

In the larger cities, such as Shanghai, Nanjing, Wuhan, and Xian, students march in the streets. At Nankai University in Tianjin, which is about seventeen miles from Beijing, several hundred students decide to go to the capital, but university authorities stop them by canceling their train tickets. However, thirty-six graduate students successfully pass themselves off to Beijing as workers. They are the first group of students to enter Beijing from other parts of the country.

The authorities of Beijing University refuse to give the names of student leaders to the police.

April 22, Saturday
Students Kneeling for Democracy

A memorial service is held in the Great Hall of the People while police stand guard outside. First, on the preceding night, students from nineteen colleges established a provisional committee to organize student attendance at the memorial service at Tiananmen Square the next morning. Alarmed authorities moved troops from the suburbs into the city overnight, and by five o'clock this morning the police and the army had taken positions on all sides of the Square. Meanwhile, more than two hundred thousand students and some other citizens arrive at the Square; they sit on the ground and wait quietly for the memorial service. Deputies of the provision committee negotiate with the authorities for three requests: to guarantee the safety of the sit-in students in the Square; to allow students to enter the Great Hall to pay their respects to Hu's remains; and to acknowledge the fact that armed police beat students in the April 20 Xinhuamen Gate incident. By six A.M., the officials accept only the first request of the three. At eight A.M. police cordon off Tiananmen Square; the memorial service starts at ten A.M., and the proceedings are

broadcast through loudspeakers to the Square. When the band begins to play the national anthem, two hundred thousand voices join in a splendid mixed chorus on Tiananmen Square. The memorial service goes smoothly, and the Square is filled with a solemn silence. At 12:10 P.M. the cordon is removed; the students begin to shout slogans demanding a dialogue with Premier Li Peng.

At the memorial service for Hu Yaobang, a grand ceremony in the Great Hall of the People, President Yang Shangkun presides. General Secretary Zhao Ziyang gives the memorial speech; senior leader Deng Xiaoping attends the service. Others present include Li Peng, Wan Li, Peng Zheng, Nie Rongzhen, Qiao Shi, Hu Qili, Yao Yilin, and Wang Zhen. About four thousand top Party and government officials attend the ceremony.

At 12:04 P.M., escorted by Qiao Shi, Hu Qili, Song Ping, Wen Jiabao, and Hu Yaobang's widow Li Zhao and their sons and daughters, the hearse carrying Hu's remains comes out from the western door of the Great Hall and heads to Babaoshan

Cemetery. In silence, more than a million mourners stand in line on both sides of the city's main streets leading to the cemetery to pay their last respects to the former leader.

After the ceremony, the sit-in students send three representatives to the front door of the Great Hall to deliver a petition to Premier Li Peng. To request Li Peng to come out, one of the students goes down on his knees and puts the petition on his head. Another of the three is Wuer Kaixi, a freshman at Beijing Normal University, who does not kneel down. Since Li Peng never shows up, the three students withdraw

from the steps of the Great Hall at 1:30 P.M. When the students leave Tiananmen Square that afternoon, the Beida Preparatory Committee of the Solidarity Student Union warns that if the government continues to ignore the students' requests, the Preparatory Committee will call for a general strike of workers, peasants, and intellectuals throughout the country.

Memorial meetings for Hu Yaobang are held in other cities in the country, and in Hong Kong, Macao, and Chinese embassies abroad as well.

The photograph is surrounded by the words, "Crying for freedom, kneeling for democracy," and "The Republic will never forget."

Students kneel on the steps of the People's Great Hall, asking to meet Premier Li Peng.

14

New China News Agency's Hong Kong branch decorates mourning hall for Yaobang.

Hu Deping, the oldest son of Hu Yaobang, keeps vigil beside bier with his family in the mourning hall in Hu's residence.

Zhao Ziyang's Memorial Speech at the Ceremony in Condolence of Comrade Hu Yaobang

Today, laden with extreme pain and sorrow, we gather here to mourn Comrade Hu Yaobang, a long-tested loyal fighter for Communism, a great proletarian revolutionary, a great statesman, a prominent political commissar of the people's army and an outstanding leader who held important posts in the Party for many years.

As a Marxist, Comrade Hu Yaobang's life was a glorious one. In his sixty-year revolutionary career, he was absolutely faithful to the Party and the people, exerting his utmost efforts through hard struggles to confer—and surely he did confer—lasting benefits on the Party and the people. So we all look with profound grief upon his death, as a great loss to the Party and the people, a great loss to China's socialist modernization.

Ever since his teens, Comrade Hu Yaobang devoted himself to our new democratic revolution. He was born on November 20, 1915, in a poor peasant family in Liuyang County, Hunan Province. He became a member of the Chinese Communist Youth League in 1929, and then in 1933 he joined the Chinese Communist Party. At that time he was mainly engaged in propaganda work among youths in the revolutionary base areas in Jiangxi, Hunan, and Fujian provinces and fought with the local feudal forces and Kuomingtang reactionaries. In 1934 he joined in the Long March of the Red Army and was wounded in the siege of Loushan Pass; some bullet fragments still remain in his body. After the Red Army arrived in northern Shaanxi, he was appointed to the position of secretary general and then as head of the Bureau of the Chinese Communist Party. During the War of Resistance against Japanese Aggression, he held the posts of head of the Department of Organization and of the General Political Department of the Military Commission of the Central Committee of the Chinese Communist Party. During the War of Liberation, he was deputy director of the Political Department of the Hebei-Rehe-Liaoning Military Area, political commissar of the Third and Fourth Columns of the Shaanxi-Chahaer-Hebei Military Area, and then head of the Political Department of the 18th Army. He participated in the campaign to safeguard Zhangjiako and the campaigns to liberate Shijiazhuand, Taiyuan, and Baoji, thereby making important contributions to the final victories of those wars.

After the founding of the People's Republic in 1949, Comrade Hu Yaobang was first appointed to the posts of secretary of the Party Committee, director of the Administrative Committee, and military commissar of the Northern Sichuan Area. Under his leadership, both land reform and the campaign to suppress bandits and despots were successful, and industrial and agricultural production in this region underwent a swift recovery and growth. From 1952 on, he served over a lengthy period of time on the Central Committee of the Communist Youth League of China, first as secretary and later as first secretary. This period saw his creative implementation of the Party's instructions among the young people; it was the most active and productive period since the establishment of the People's Republic. Particularly notable is the fact that he gave full attention to educating the young, to carrying out a rich variety of activities that met the needs of the young, and to advocating a philosophy of work that was "lively and vigorous, practical and realistic." Consequently, the Youth League became popular among the young and played an important role in organizing them to fulfill the tasks given to them by the Party. Since the end of 1964, Hu Yaobang has been secretary of the Party Committee of the Northwest Region and first secretary of the Party Committee of Shaanxi Province. He has immersed himself in the masses and carried out many construction programs in the region.

During the so-called "Great Cultural Revolution," Comrade Hu Yaobang suffered severe persecution, which he resisted at the cost of his personal safety. Throughout those horrible years he carried on an unswerving struggle against the counter-revolutionary cliques headed by Lin Biao and Jiang Qing. In 1975, when he held a leading position at the Chinese Academy of Science, he resolutely opposed the sabotage carried on by Jiang Qing and her like.

After the downfall of the gang headed by Jiang Qing, Comrade Hu Yaobang successively held the posts of vice president of the Central Committee of the Chinese Communist Party, third secretary of the Disciplinary Inspection Committee of the Central Party Committee, secretary of the Central Party Committee, and concurrent head of the Department of Propaganda. He was a member of the eighth, eleventh, twelfth, and thirteenth CCP Central Committees; he was elected to the Political Bureau of the CCP Central Committee. At the Fifth Plenary Session of the Eleventh CCP Central Committee, he was elected a member of the Standing Committee of the Political Bureau of the CCP Central Committee and general secretary of the Committee. He was a member of the Political Bureau as well as a member of its Standing Committee of the Twelfth CCP Central Committee. After the Second Plenary Session of the Twelfth CCP Central Committee, he held the position of director of the Central Guiding Committee for Party Reform. And he was general secretary of the CCP Central

Dead is the upright official; in power are the corrupt; hundreds and thousands of people are upset. The banner says: "Down with the corrupt officials."

Committee from September 1982 through January 1987.

The Third Session of the Eleventh CCP Central Committee marked the beginning of a new important historical period of reform. In the report presented at the Twelfth CCP National Congress on behalf of the Central Committee, Comrade Hu Yaobang explicitly reiterated the Party guidelines for the new era. He plunged himself over the past eleven years into tremendous efforts to combine the fundamental principles of Marxism with its practice in China's modernization. He adhered to the Party line that followed the Third Plenary Session of the Eleventh CCP Central Committee; he adhered to the four essential principles and the policy of reform and being open to the world in China's pursuit of socialism with her own features; his contributions are manifold and of great value.

Showing unusual courage, he did much to redress past injustices based on false charges and to implement the Party's policies on cadres so as to enable the deposed veteran cadres to regain leadership, and a large number of cadres, intellectuals, and civilians wronged for many a year were rehabilitated.

Giving full attention to arousing enthusiasm among China's eight hundred million peasants, he managed the formulation and implementation of a series of agricultural reform policies, which eventually brought about a rapid growth in our agricultural economy.

Hu Yaobang with the Tibetan children, June 1980, Lhasa.

17

His attention was also given to the workers. The document entitled "CCP Central Committee's Decision Concerning Reform of China's Economic Structure" was prepared and issued under his direction and was meant to start an overall reform of our economic structure with cities as the key point. He spared no effort in opening the coastal regions to the world.

He respected knowledge and talent, always attending to the Party's responsibilities in the fields of science, education, art and literature, and journalism. In his speeches on the development of China's young intellectuals, he repeatedly and most enthusiastically encouraged them to go down to grass-roots units and live among the masses to be tempered and simultaneously make contributions in the practice of our socialist modernization. For this purpose, two documents of great importance were put into practice, i.e., "CCP Central Committee's Decision about Reform of the Educational System" and "CCP Central Committee's Resolution of the Guiding-Line in the Spiritual Construction of Socialist Civilization."

At the meeting held by the CCP Central Committee to commemorate the centenary of the death of Karl Marx, he delivered a lengthy speech entitled "The Brilliant Light of the Great Truth of Marxism Illuminates Our Road," in which he testified to our Party's firm commitment to following and developing Marxism under new historical circumstances. He tirelessly endeavored to improve the construction of ideology, work style, discipline, and organization within the Party as well as to press on with the reform of the cadre system and the replacement of senior leaders with younger, qualified ones at all levels.

He also made considerable attempts to restore and develop the relationship between the CCP and other communist and workers' parties, to develop the relationship between the CCP and foreign social, nationalist, or other parties, to promote mutual understanding and friendship between the Chinese people and various governments and peoples in the world, and to adjust our foreign policies for the new historical period.

Comrade Hu Yaobang dedicated his whole life to our cause. He loved the Party and the people profoundly, and the Party and the people loved him profoundly. The Party and nation mourn him. We are determined to learn from his revolutionary spirit and his ideas and virtues.

We should all learn from his total dedication to the Party's cause, from his devotion to Communism, from his strong sense of revolutionary obligation, and political responsibility, and from his untiring service to the people. Over the past two years, he demonstrated wholehearted concern for reform and modernization.

We should all learn from his close ties with the masses. He made friends with people from all walks of life. He made several trips into former revolutionary base areas, districts inhabited by minor nationalities, remote and poverty-stricken regions, where he had heart-to-heart talks with both local cadres and the common folks and discussed with them plans to rid the country of poverty and speed up economical development. He also paid many visits to the frontiers and coastal border, getting to know the soldiers. Apart from all this, while he had plenty of state affairs to tackle, he personally read and answered thousands of letters from the masses.

We should all learn from his consideration, his honesty and modesty, from his placement of the Party and the people above all, from his adherence to the right and his self-criticism when he realized his mistakes, from his self-discipline, his kindness to others, his democratic work style, his eagerness to learn, and his continual efforts to achieve more for the cause of Communism.

Comrade Hu Yaobang has left us. We should turn our grief into strength and continue what he had yet to accomplish. With one mind and one heart, let us unite and stand more closely with the Central Committee of the Communist Party of China, ready to work hard for, and forge ahead towards our glorious goal—the realization of socialist modernization. Comrades, let us work hard and struggle through to the end!

Eternal glory to Comrade Hu Yaobang!

April 23, Sunday
Xian and Changsha Hit by Riots

Xian: In the afternoon of April 22, thousands of students and other people gather at Xincheng Square in front of Shaanxi provincial government in mourning of Hu Yaobang. Lawbreakers, moving through the crowd shouting anti-government slogans, clash with police while attempting to force their way into the government compound. They set fire to a janitor's room, a reception room, and a truck at the gate. The students, alarmed by the violence, withdraw from the Square. The riots continue until the evening. The lawbreakers push over the western wall of the government compound and dash into the provincial court and procurators' offices. They set fire to five cars and the garage, an oil depot, and some buses, and they also loot shops. Police arrest eighteen looters and suppress the riot. More than thirty students and a hundred policemen are injured.

Changsha seven P.M.: April 22, after public broadcasts of a memorial service for Hu Yaobang in May First Square of Changsha, the capital city of Hunan province, rioters smash a car and a police box in the Square and plunder shops until midnight. Several hundred armed police finally get the situation under control by morning. About one hundred arrests are made; most of those arrested are hooligans with criminal records, the police say, and none are students.

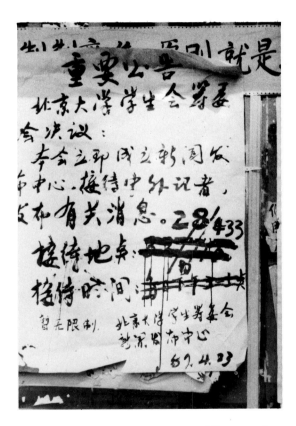

Beida students initiate a news center to deliver news to Chinese and foreign reporters, April 23.

College student representatives head for Beijing intending to form a national student organization. First, twenty-one colleges in Beijing establish a "Federation of All-Beijing College Student Unions (Interim)" (FBSUI),

Beida students raise money for the student movement.

19

including Beida, Qinghua, People's University, Science and Technology, Political Science and Law, Finance and Economics, Aeronautical Engineering, Central Nationalities, Beijing Normal, and other colleges of sciences, agriculture, medicine, and education. As more and more students from Tianjin, Shanghai, Wuhan, Hunan, and other areas enter Beijing, a national federation of student unions is considered. In the meantime, initiated by Beida, students begin to raise money for their organizations.

At Kim Il Sung's invitation, General Secretary Zhao Ziyang leaves Beijing in the afternoon by train on his visit to North Korea. Zhao's schedule remains the same despite the student movement. Zhao's entourage includes Foreign Minister Wu Xueqian, Hong Xuezhi, Zhu Liang, and Liu Shuqing. Premier Li Peng, Qiao Shi, Tian Jiyun, Wen Jiabao, and Chi Haotian go to the railway station to see Zhao off.

April 24, Monday

The FBSUI declares a "no limit class boycott" in thirty-five colleges in Beijing to protest police atrocities in the Xinhuamen Gate incident and censorship of the news. The students ask for their teachers' understanding of their fight for democracy and freedom, and they receive the support of the faculty of Beida and the People's University, and other intellectuals. At the same time, more than one hundred groups of students go to the streets to tell people that the student movement is for "democracy, freedom, human rights, rule of law, and modernization," and that the movement is going on in a reasonable and constitutional way. The students also raise money on the streets to finance their movement.

The April 23 issue of the *Science and Technology Daily News* reports the student movement and thus breaks through the censorship imposed on journalism for forty years in mainland China. The fourth page of the newspaper is filled with photographs of student demonstrations, and an article on page two covers the real story of the movement by asserting that democracy and freedom are the aims of the campaign. It is rumored that the newspaper has been under pressure from the authorities. In the intense debate during the night, it is said, Sun Changjiang, the first deputy editor-in-chief, and other editors and reporters have threatened to resign if the paper does not cover the demonstration, and that this confrontation has caused the delay in publication. The next day, students vie with each

Science and Technology Daily News *reports the student movement.*

Deputy editor-in-chief of the Science and Technology Daily News *Sun Changjiang has the courage to tell the truth.*

other to read the newspaper and put up posters saluting the *Science and Technology Daily News*.

A poster on the campus of Beida. The center announcement calls for a general strike on April 27 in the name of the FBSUI.

Hong Kong's student union federation sends its deputies to Beijing several days before to observe the student movement. The deputies meet Rong Kang, head of the second department of the Hong Kong–Macau office under the State Council, and request a meeting with members of the Standing Committee of the National People's Congress (NPC). They also visit those colleges most involved, such as Beida, People's University, and some others. In Hong Kong, members of the "April Fifth Action" organization go to the local branch of Xinhua (New China News Agency) demanding that the Chinese government open dialogue with students on democratic reform and rule of law.

A poster with a list of relatives of high officials appears on the campuses of Beida and Qinghua. Twenty-seven names are on the list, including Deng Xiaoping's son Deng Pufang, Zhao Ziyang's oldest son Zhao Dajun, Yang Shangkun's younger brother Yang Baibing, Yang Shangkun's son-in-law Chi Haotian, Wan Li's son-in-law Li Ruikuan, Wang Zhen's son Wang Jun, Po Yipo's son Po Xilai, etc.; most of these twenty-seven occupy positions of power. The poster demands that the government make known the properties of those in the list and investigate corruptions and *guandao*. Copies of the poster spread quickly on other campuses.

April 25, Tuesday

A dialogue between government officials and Qinghua students scheduled on Tuesday does not take place because of severe criticism from the students of many other colleges. The dialogue has been arranged by Yuan Chunqing, secretary general of the authorized All-China Federation of Student Unions, who has invited the officials of the State Council, the Beijing Municipal Government, and the Higher Education Ministry to meet with representatives of the authorized Student Union of Qinghua University.

For days the authorities cut off the telephone service in Beida student dormitories and the telegram bureau refuses to send telegrams to colleges outside of Beijing; there are also rumors that the thirty-eighth infantry stationed at Baoding and the garrison force in Shaanxi are moving into Beijing; the students are increasingly uneasy. On April 25 one hundred thousand students on strike pour into the streets to ask for the support of the people. There are crowds everywhere. Transportation is at a standstill. On the campuses of Qinghua and the University of Political Science and Law, students burn copies of the *People's Daily*, the *Beijing Daily*, and *Qiushi* magazine to protest false reporting of the news, to demand freedom of the press, and to demand dialogues with the government.

The *Economic Herald* incident: The Shanghai-based *World Economic Herald* reports a gathering in Hu Yaobang's memory in its April 24 issue. According to the report, some speakers at the meeting claimed that the Central Committee of the CCP made a mistake when it dismissed Hu as general secretary of the Party in 1987. Jiang Zemin, then party secretary of Shanghai Municipal Committee and also a member of the Political Bureau of the CCP, orders three hundred thousand printed copies of the newspaper confiscated and demands that the editors replace the report with other articles and reprint the issue. Qin Benli, the editor-in-chief, ignores the order

to write a new filler and leaves a blank in the reprinted issue to show that something has been censored. The new April 24 issue of the *Economic Herald* with its blank space is the most exciting news of the day throughout the country. The *Herald* incident and the *Science and Technology Daily News'* honest coverage of the student movement are significant breaks in the censorship that has been imposed by the government for so long.

A hundred and fifty-nine faculty members of the People's University sign a letter in support of student movement. The letter points out that the official newspapers' reports of the student movement are inconsistent with the facts, have sullied the students' reputation and violated their legal rights. It requests that the *People's Daily*, the CCTV, and other official institutions apologize to the students and support the movement. For days, professors and lecturers

Striking students making propaganda on streets, asking for freedom of the press.

give speeches in favor of the movement and are warmly welcomed by the students.

To gain support from other parts of the country, the Federation of All-Beijing College Student Unions initiates a "one person, ten letters" action to break the news block and to get their information circulated across the country. In addition, the FBSUI tries to collect enough money to send two or three hundred deputies to fifteen cities, to speak for the democratic movement and organize a nationwide student strike on May 4. It is hoped that the strike will begin new democracy in China.

According to rumor, the Political Bureau of the Central Committee met some days before and decided to open a dialogue with representatives of the authorized student unions, but not the "illegal" student organizations. Another unconfirmed news story indicates that Deng Xiaoping intends to use harsh measures and has issued

The student organization calls for students to hold out in their struggle for democracy.

In late April, while students are still mourning Hu's death, armed police show up on Tiananmen Square.

instructions to repress the student movement no matter what the bloodshed. In the evening, the CCTV televises an advance of the April 26 editorial of the *People's Daily*, claiming that the student movement has stirred up turmoil.

April 26, Wednesday
People's Daily *Editorial Claiming Student Movement Turmoil*

The *People's Daily* publishes an editorial under the title, "Take a Clear-Cut Stand against Unrest." It claims that "a handful of people with ulterior motives have continued to use the grief of students to create turmoil. . . . Their purpose is to poison people's minds, create national turmoil, and sabotage the nation's political stability. This is a planned conspiracy which, in essence, aims at negating the leadership of the Party and the socialist system." The editorial calls on "the Party and the nation to recognize the gravity of the situation and unite in a stand against public disturbances, to protect China's political stability."

Party Secretary of Beijing Municipal Committee Li Ximing says that the students are stirring up trouble by using the methods of the Cultural Revolution and that the student movement should be stopped. Chen Xitong, the mayor, relays Deng Xiaoping's instruction; he also warns of "black hands" behind the students.

The Central Committee of the CCP musters the 38th Army into the capital from Baoding, not far from Beijing. The 38th infantry is considered the elite guard of the CCP Central Committee. It is reported that at least twenty thousand troops move into the city.

The editorial of April 26 of the People's Daily *claims the student movement is a disturbance.*

After the death of Hu Yaobang, the Federation of Beijing College Student Unions gradually united student organizations of forty-one colleges in Beijing and became the policy-making body for the student movement. In the face of the policy declared by the government, the FBSUI now responds with a press conference on the campus of China University of Political Science and Law in the afternoon of April 26. Seven leaders of the FBSUI are introduced to the students and three demands are raised again: 1) The government should hold dialogues with students on the basis of equality; 2) The April 20 Xinhuamen Gate incident should be investigated, responsibility for it should be affixed, the Public Security Ministry should apologize to the students for the police's beating of students, and newspapers should publish true reports of the incident; 3) New China

News Agency and other official news media should faithfully report the story of the student movement. The FBSUI emphasizes the commitment of the organization to peaceful and legal means to pursue the goals of democracy, freedom, human rights, rule of law, and modernization. The Federation finally announces a mammoth demonstration for the next day to protest the editorial of the *People's Daily* that calls the student movement a cause of "turmoil."

On hearing plans for the demonstration, the Beijing Municipal Public Security Bureau declares the mourning activities for Hu Yaobang ended and forbids demonstrations without permission; public speech, raising money, and distributing leaflets on the street are also forbidden; violators will be punished.

The Peaceful Petition Organization Committee of Qinghua University, the lead-

Students from the University of Political Science and Law protest that it is unconstitutional for the Public Security Bureau to forbid the students' demonstration.

ing body of the Qinghua student movement, suddenly withdraws from the FBSUI
and disbands on April 26. At the same time,
the newborn Student Liaison Office on
Qinghua Campus also decides not to participate in the demonstration, saying that the
demonstration might throw a scare into
middle-of-the-roaders and lose their support, and also that the demonstration could
cause bloodshed. Students discuss this
development all around the campus; some
accuse their leaders of being weak and
demand new leadership.

The Shanghai Municipal Committee of
the CCP convenes a meeting to brief the
city's forty thousand Party cadres and officials about the April 26 editorial of the
People's Daily.

*Qinghua students were the main force of the movement,
but suddenly their leaders withdraw from FBSUI on
April 26.*

People's Daily editorial on April 26, 1989
"An Urgent Call for a Firm Stand against Turmoil"

*During the days of mourning for Comrade
Hu Yaobang, great numbers of Communists,
workers, peasants, intellectuals, office workers,
PLA soldiers, and young students used various
forms to express their sadness. They resolved to
transform their sorrow into strength and strive
to realize the four modernizations to make a
stronger China.*

*During that period, however, a handful of
people in Beijing fabricated rumors against the
leaders of the Party and the government. They
incited people to storm into Zhongnanhai from
Xinhuamen where the headquarters of the
Central Party Committee and the State Council
are located. A few even shouted for the overthrow of the Chinese Communist Party. In Xian
and Changsha, rioters looted shops, smashed
public properties, beat people, and burned vehicles.*

*Considering that the majority of the people
were in mourning, and that youngsters may
overreact when they are excited, the Party and
the government exercised the utmost restraint
and tolerance. On April 22, the memorial for*

*Hu Yaobang was held as scheduled; however, the
government did not insist on the students'
clearance from the Square as it customarily
would. Instead, the students were asked to keep
order and join in the memorial service. Because
both sides made an effort, the service was carried out in the required atmosphere of solemnity.*

*Nevertheless, right after the meeting a hand-
ful of individuals with ulterior motives went on
making use of the young students' emotional
feelings about Hu Yaobang to create rumors,
confuse people's thinking, and write pamphlets
and large character posters slandering the Party
and government leaders. They openly went
against the constitution of the country by opposing the leadership of the Communist Party and
socialist system. In some of the universities and
colleges, illegal organizations were set up, announcing that they were going to "seize the
power" from the legal student unions. Some
forced their way into the university broadcasting rooms. They incited faculty and students to
boycott class; they even blocked the way to class-
rooms for their fellow students. They also*

printed, in the worker's name, counter-revolutionary handbills and traveled to get more supporters in an attempt to stir up an even bigger disturbance.

These facts make it clear that this handful of individuals were not mourning Hu Yaobang, nor were they working to push the process of the socialist democratic politics in China. They were not just letting off steam. They were waving the flag of democracy to violate democratic principles; their purpose was to instigate dissension between the party and the people, create national disorder, and sabotage the stable unity in politics that China has been enjoying for years. This is a plotted conspiracy, an upheaval to negate from a fundamental basis the leadership of the Chinese Communist Party and the socialist system. The whole nation and the whole party are facing a serious political challenge.

If the unrest is not handled quickly, we will soon face a very grave time of confusion and disorder. In that case, the things that the people hope to achieve—such as the open policy, order and construction, price control, improvement of life, eliminating corruption, and developing a better system of democracy and law—will all become impossible. We may lose all the great achievements that we gained during the ten years of reform, let alone the realization of the plan of a stronger China. It is possible that a hopeful, promising country will become a hopeless, agitated country.

All the members of the Party and all nationalities in China must fully understand the graveness of the struggle. We must unite and stand firmly in opposing the turmoil. We must protect the constitution and socialist democracy and law and resolutely defend the hard-earned political stability and unity. No illegal organizations are allowed in China. Any excuses to violate the rights of the legal student unions will be denied. Rumor mongers should be punished in accordance with criminal law. No illegal demonstrations. No visiting of students to the factories, countrysides, or schools. Those who commit violence will be prosecuted. Students have the right to go to school, and that right should be protected. Many students wish to wipe out corruption and promote democracy, which are also the Party's and the government's intentions. However, these can only be fulfilled under the leadership of the Party through reforms and better socialist democratic laws.

Comrades of the whole party and people of the whole nation must see clearly that China will be in agony if this turmoil is not ended. This struggle means the life or death of the open policy and of the four modernizations. And for China's future. Party organizations at all levels, all the members of the Party, of the Youth League, of all the Chinese democratic parties, all patriots must differentiate right from wrong, must stand firm and eliminate the turmoil resolutely and immediately.

Hundreds of thousands of students and citizens peacefully sit on the Square, showing their hunger for democracy. This was called a disturbance.

April 27, Thursday
Escalation of the Student Movement

The FBSUI-sponsored demonstration, the biggest in the history of the People's Republic, takes place in Beijing. From eight in the morning, about two hundred thousand students from forty-two colleges march twenty-five miles on the city's main streets, passing before Tiananmen Gate and breaking through eighteen police lines formed by uniformed bodies. Both students and police exercise great restraint, and no clash is reported. Military vehicles sometimes stalk among the crowd and students cheer the soldiers and shake hands with them. Every time they break police line the students shout "People's police have the love of the people" or "We salute the police," as citizens around clap their hands and shout slogans with the students. More than a million people crowd both sides of the streets to cheer the students and bring food and drink to them; the scene is deeply moving. In front of the procession are members of the FBSUI, including Wuer Kaixi, and the procession of each college is led by its student leaders. To prevent non-student elements from mixing into the procession and creating unwanted incidents, students hold hands with each other on both sides of the parade when they march. The banners and posters held by the demonstrators say "Peaceful petition is not turmoil," "Support the leadership of the Chinese Communist Party," "Down with the *guandao*," "Long live Democracy," "Down with 'rule by individuals,' long live the 'rule of law,'" "Freedom of the press." The demonstration lasts fourteen hours, then the students return to their campuses to celebrate. Before the demonstration, some students thought they might be repressed by armed police, so they left wills behind; now they put up banners reading "Thank you, Beijing citizens"

The army and police make up a wall of human bodies trying to stop the mammoth demonstration.

The locking of arms at student marches keeps the procession in order.

and "History will never forget April 27."

In the afternoon, State Council spokesman Yuan Mu announces that "1) We welcome the students into direct dialogues with us, for the Party and government have always stood for dialogue between the government and the broad masses and have already had various exchanges with them through different channels. Students asked for dialogues to get their opinions to us, and this is exactly what we would like to do. 2) There has to be a suitable atmosphere for such dialogue and all talks must be conducted through appropriate channels. We are ready to talk to students at any time, but we demand that students go back to school, pass their opinions through proper channels, and adopt a calm and reasonable attitude. Otherwise, it will remain difficult for them to obtain their goals. 3) The State Council has entrusted the All-China and Beijing Municipal Students' Federations to

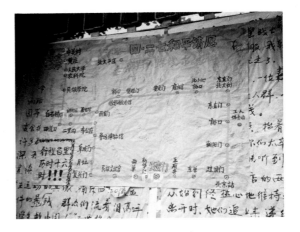

Students try to avoid disorder in advance, telling their fellows what to do if somebody tries to disturb the peaceful demonstration.

The banners say, "Reform and Be Open," "News should tell the truth."

The banner says, "Take a clear-cut stand; oppose the editorial of April 26."

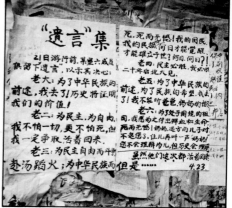

Students leave wills before they go to the demonstration.

forward the students' demands and sponsor talks with the appropriate authorities in good time."

The petition initiated by the famous poet Beidao and supported by forty-seven others now circulates among the intellectuals, and more than two hundred well-known scholars sign their names.

In Changsha, the capital city of Hunan province, order returns for several days after the April 23 riots. Stirred by the *People's Daily* editorial, however, two thousand students take to the street in a demonstration on April 27. In the afternoon, the students dash into the provincial government building demanding dialogue with

The procession breaks up eighteen cordons of police.

Taking pictures.

April 27, 1989, will never be forgotten.

Two hundred thousand students and one million citizens trap the armed police in a sea of people.

the authorities. At five P.M., officials announce through loudspeakers that the leaders of the provincial government will talk to the students the next morning. The students then withdraw from the building.

Some hundred Hong Kong college students gather before the front door of the Xinhua (New China News Agency) Hong Kong branch in the morning asking to meet the Xinhua officials, and tear copies of the editorial of the April 26 *People's Daily* to

show their anger. At eleven A.M. the deputy secretary of the Xinhua branch Yang Sheng meets ten student representatives and accepts their "Statement"; he also promises to communicate it to the top levels. That afternoon, some two hundred students gather at the door and put up placards supporting the student movement in Beijing; the protestors remain there until evening, when they learn of the victory of the demonstration in Beijing. Before they leave, the protestors cut their fingers and drop their blood in turn to produce two posters reading "Glory to the student movement, long live the Democracy," and "Love of country is not criminal; repression of students is a shame." The secretary of the Hong Kong Student Federation, T'ao Chunhsing, announces that these posters will be sent to Beijing student organizations.

The University of Taiwan student union and news agency announce a statement calling on all Taiwan students to support the student movement in mainland China and putting forward three demands to the governments on both sides of the Taiwan Straits: 1) to return autonomy to colleges and guarantee the independence of scholarship, and to clean up Party influence on campuses; 2) to give up all sorts of actions in opposition to democracy and freedom, to be open to all kinds of opinions about refor-

mation, and to reform the mechanisms of government; 3) to release dissenters from imprisonment.

In England, sixty-five Chinese intellectuals at twelve colleges appeal to overseas Chinese to promote democratic reform in China by voicing their opinions. In Hong Kong, thirty-five college teachers call on the masses to pay close attention to the Beijing student movement and appeal to both the Chinese government and the student demonstrators to exercise restraint.

The Shanghai Party Municipal Committee dismisses Qin Benli from his position as the editor-in-chief of the *World Economic Herald* on the charge of violating Party discipline in publishing the report of the forum in Hu Yaobang's memory. The staff members of the newspaper disagree with the Party's decision and visit Qin Benli in his home to express their sympathy.

April 28, Friday
Wuer Kaixi Chairs the FBSU

The Federation of Beijing Student Unions (Interim) (FBSUI) decides to disband and to reform as the Federation of Beijing Student Unions (FBSU) when it meets in Beijing Normal University in the afternoon. Representatives from more than forty colleges attend the meeting. Through discussions and secret ballots, the meeting accepts the resignation of Zhou Yongjun, a student of the University of Political Science and Law and chairman of the former FBSUI, elects Wuer Kaixi, a twenty-one-year-old Uygur student of the Beijing Normal, as chairman of the Federation and elects a Standing Committee composed of six members from Beida, People's University, Beijing Normal, Political Science and Law, Central Nationalities, and the fine arts colleges. Wuer Kaixi declares that the Federation will provide leadership to Beijing autonomous student unions and will coexist with the authorized All-China Students' Federation. But he also warns that the authorities assert the FBSU to be illegal, that they have

already named several of its members on charges of planning to overthrow the government and stirring up reactionary disturbance, and that these could be arrested at any time.

Yuan Chunqing, secretary general of the authorized All-China Students' Federation, tells newsmen that the State Council has agreed to talk to the students and that he believes the dialogue will take place soon. But Yuan also says that the students should show their good faith in the dialogue and that demonstrations and class boycotts are unreasonable actions. Yuan announces that the All-China and Beijing Students' Federations have already set up a reception office and hot-line numbers to gather student opinions.

Wuer Kaixi expresses the Federation's good faith and its call for dialogue with the government. According to an investigation on campuses, Wuer Kaixi says, the students have agreed on three points: 1) The dialogue shall be widely reported through the

Twenty-one-year-old student leader Wuer Kaixi enjoys the support of the students.

official news media. 2) Student leaders, including officers of the FBSU and leaders of each Autonomous Student Union, shall not be prosecuted "after the autumn harvest" (i.e., when all this is over). 3) The authorities should be fair and honest in dealing with the student movement. As to the dialogue, the students have a sevenpoint agenda; they will ask that the authorities: 1) regard Hu Yaobang's work as positive and affirm democracy and freedom; 2) reject the two party-sponsored campaigns of "opposing bourgeois democracy" and "cleaning up bourgeois mental pollution"; 3) open the properties of the high officials of the Party and the government, and that of their relatives as well; 4) guarantee freedom of the press and allow unauthorized newspapers to exist; 5) increase the budget for education and raise intellectuals' salaries; 6) lift bans on peaceful demonstrations; 7) report the real story of the student movement. Wuer Kaixi says that the dialogue should start as soon as possible, no later than the

May 4 anniversary, so as to avoid a split among the students. The FBSU also declares a signature drive on the various campuses in order to prove itself the legitimate representative of the students and thus urge the government to recognize it as a legal organization.

In the United States, Press Secretary Marlin Fitzwater says of Beijing that President Bush "deeply believes that the principles of freedom of speech and the right of assembly are in place there." Fitzwater says, "We hope that the demonstration will remain peaceful and the Chinese authorities will exercise restraint in dealing with the events. . . . Students have the right to protest and speak out in their pursuit of democracy and freedom. We support the students' petition." But he has

no comment on the demands of the students. "We are not sure that we understand," he says, "what the students are asking for."

Tianjin: On April 24, students at many campuses begin class boycotts. The afternoon of April 28, six thousand students take to the streets shouting "support the Chinese Communist Party," "uphold the four basic principles" (The four basic principles, initiated by Deng Xiaoping, are adherence to the leadership of the Chinese Communist Party, to the socialist system, to the people's democratic dictatorship, and to Marxist, Leninist, and Maoist thought), "down with corrupted officials," and "journalism should tell the truth." The march remains orderly, with police help.

Linking arms, the policemen try to keep order.

April 29, Saturday
General Secretary Zhao Ziyang Returns to Beijing

At the invitation of All-China and Beijing Students' Federations, State Council spokesman Yuan Mu, Vice-Minister of the State Education Commission He Dongchang, Secretary General of the Beijing Municipal Party Committee Yuan Liben, and Vice-Mayor Lu Yuchen attend a "dialogue forum" in the afternoon and meet forty-five students from sixteen colleges in Beijing. The students state that they are attending the forum as individuals, not as representatives of their schools. The talks last for about three hours and are televised in detail. State Council spokesman Yuan Mu says that Premier Li Peng hopes the students will resume their classes as soon as possible and express their opinions through proper channels. Several students leave the meeting, saying that it cannot solve any problems because Party and State leaders are absent and because the students present cannot represent their schools as they were not elected by their schoolmates. Wuer Kaixi was invited but told not to talk, so he refuses to be present. He tells reporters that the "forum" is not a "dialogue" at all, but a trick of the government to destroy student solidarity, and that the FBSU will persist in asking for a real dialogue with the government and the good faith of the government.

In spite of being considered an illegal organization by the authorities, the FBSU works on the preparation for the seventieth anniversary of the May Fourth movement and declares a continuation of class boycotts, and initiates the *News Report*. The first issue, published on April 29, covers the movement over the past two weeks. In the meantime, on the campus of Qinghua University, students establish a "dialogue preparatory committee" to collect and summarize students' requests for dialogue with the government.

In Hong Kong, for days, statements in support of the Beijing student movement have come from ten unions, ten Christian groups, fifteen syndicated youth unions, and students' unions at eight colleges.

Zhao Ziyang, then the general secretary of the CCP.

General Secretary of the CCP Zhao Ziyang returns to Beijing after an official visit to North Korea. China watchers believe that the Political Bureau of the Central Committee has met for several days and has been waiting for Zhao's return to take action to end the student movement.

Yuan Mu, the government spokesman.

35

Dialogue between Yuan Mu, He Dongchang, and the Students
April 29, 1989 (Condensed)

YUAN MU: . . . *The leaders of the Party and government, particularly Comrade Li Peng, wanted me to inform you, and through you all the students, that the* People's Daily *editorial was not condemning you when it said "it is a serious political struggle that aims at the communist party leadership and socialist system." In fact, the editorial was referring to a very small group of individuals who took illegal actions. It was by no means against you students. You people are filled with patriotic enthusiasm and want to push democracy ahead. You want to further reform, punish bribery, and eliminate corruption. These are exactly what the Party and government want to do. . . .*

STUDENT *(from Beijing University of Aviation and Aeronautics): One of the slogans that the students shouted was "Guandao, guandao, (profiteering, profiteering)! Strike hard against it; it will not disappear by itself." That was well put because the corruption in our country is devastating. Officials profit from corruption, and so do their sons and daughters. The Central Committee has stressed the problem many times; however, we are hearing more of thunder than of rain, that is, more of announcement than performance. We resent this. We strongly request that the government take a firm stand. We must punish those enterprises and individuals that are involved in bribery, smuggling, or any kind of violation of economic regulations.*

YUAN MU: *I do not think that* guandao *can be eliminated by striking out at it. We need to do two things to achieve that. One is for you to report what you know about a particular case. Whoever has information should let us know it. Nowadays, in almost all the cities, there is a reporting center set up by the local procuratorate. People can go there and tell what they know. I know that the Party and the government will examine these cases seriously.*

STUDENT *(from Chinese University of Law and Politics): I have two points to make. One is a statement. The dialogue is supposed to be carried out between the State Council and the representatives of the university students. But the students present at the meeting today do not seem to represent other students. We come from*

only sixteen schools and we were not elected by our fellow students. Therefore, I consider this meeting only an opportunity to create a peaceful atmosphere for future dialogue. I think of this meeting as a kind of preparation to build a channel for the real dialogue that we students want. Second, we want to make three suggestions. 1) We must immediately carry out a general election in the universities in Beijing. Let each school have two representatives elected, who will come together and form a delegation. The delegation will vote for the representatives to be present at the dialogue. 2) Before the dialogue, details should be carefully worked out in regard to time, place, number of representatives, topics, manner, and the content of the conference. 3) We may want to resume class before the dialogue takes place.

YUAN MU: . . . *I think the form of dialogues can be flexible. "Dialogue" means sitting together and exchanging views in order to know each other better. I think as long as we stick to this attitude, we can always have productive dialogues. It is better than setting up conditions for the dialogues.*

STUDENT *(from Qinghua University): That the Party has problems with its reputation and corruption is clear to everyone who can see and hear. At the university, we often hear of the nepotism of high-ranking officials. A large number of children of the cadres are assigned important jobs simply because of their connections. Are there no mediocrities among them? I hope the government will respond to this question and make some reforms.*

YUAN MU: . . . *The corruption within the Party is getting more and more serious. As a whole, our party, that is to say, most of the party members are honest. I do not mean that there is no problem. If the Party were corrupt to the core, I would not support it. My trust in the Party relies on my belief in the Party as a whole. The Party's policies in the ten years of reform are correct; our country has seen fundamental changes. No one can deny that . . . .*

STUDENT *(from Beijing Industry University): I hope the newspapers will be able to cover our meetings truthfully. Don't restrict them with censorship as you usually do before and after a* conference. By the way, is there bribery of the cadres by the central government? And by their children? If there is, please make the facts known to the public.

YUAN MU: I take full responsibility for telling you that the Central Party Committee and government have decided that whoever is found to be involved in corruption, no matter of what rank, will be prosecuted. I cannot tell you which leading comrade or whose son may be the problem. It is a difficult question for me. It is difficult, not because I am not well informed on the subject, but because we are dealing with the law.

STUDENT (from Beijing Foreign Languages Institute): An important request made by the student demonstrators is that "Newspapers must tell the truth," which is widely supported by the majority of the people. Media should become the people's voice, not just the Party's mouthpiece. Between April 15 and 25, the Chinese press hardly carried any coverage of the demonstration. Among the few articles that did report the student movement, none of them gave a true account of the perfectly orderly demonstration and rally. April 26 saw some coverage, but the stories were still one-sided. We think that the censorship of news is one of the important causes of the student movement. We demand that the press provide honest coverage of the student demonstrations, and correct the make-believe accounts of the past.

YUAN MU: Somebody proposed that news censorship be canceled. I can take the responsibility to inform you that in China there is no news censorship at all. Our media is operated on an "editor responsibility" system in which the chief editor makes the judgment of what to put into the paper and what not. If there is something that he feels uncertain about, he may represent it to the relevant offices. There is no such thing as so-called censorship. Generally speaking, our newspapers enjoy the freedom guaranteed by the Constitution, and at the same time, they are restricted by the Constitution. They must be responsible for what they say to the public, so they cannot publish just whatever they hear.

STUDENT (from Beijing Posts and Telecommunications College): First, the thirty-fifth item of the Constitution stipulates that every citizen has the freedom of speech, of association, of demonstration, and so forth. But the "ten rules regulating demonstration" issued by the Beijing municipal government that restrict the freedom of demonstration in every possible way are obviously in conflict with the Constitution. Which should override the other? Second, the People's Daily in its editorial makes no distinction between the student protest in Beijing and the rioters' violence in Xian and Changsha. Would you explain why? Did Premier Li Peng know that the students were expecting him to talk to them on April 22? The hearse of Comrade Hu Yaobang did not circle Tiananmen Square as it usually would, but left by Xinhuamen Gate. Why did it do that?

YUAN MU: You are right when you say that the Constitution guarantees freedom of speech, association, demonstration, and assembly. It stipulates at the same time, however, that a citizen must not stand against the collective interests of the country. He must not impede other people's rights. The Constitution also stipulates that the provincial people's congress has the right to make local regulations in accordance with the Constitution. I think that what the Standing Committee of Beijing People's Congress did in setting up demonstration rules is consistent with the Constitution.

STUDENT (from Beijing Normal University): How is the Central Party Committee dealing with the demonstration by tens of thousands of students? Will the student organizers be punished?

HE DONGCHANG: We believe in democracy and law. If you do not violate the government's regulations and its laws, you'll be okay. This applies to everybody alike: students, teachers, everyone. You people are young, and you may have overreacted when you were excited. As an official from the Education Commission, I will suggest leniency to all the students.

YUAN MU: I agree with Comrade He Dongchang on this point. I will pass this along to the Central Committee, and act accordingly.

STUDENT (from Beijing Medical College): Comrade Yuan said earlier that the government is determined to clean up guandao. Who do you think is the worst guandao in China? And what has the government done about it?

YUAN MU: It is impossible for me to name the

37

biggest *guandao*, but I can tell you something about what the government has been doing with the new business corporations in Beijing. We have sent out quite a number of auditing groups to examine Kanghua Company, Zhongxin Company, Guangda Company, China Agricultural Investment Company, and others. The auditors have been there for some time. They are checking these companies' financial activities. . . . Premier Li Peng has said that different areas and different enterprises may use different ways of treating the outcome of the examinations. They can use news media to inform the public; they should listen to criticisms and submit to supervision. The point is not to fail in our efforts to reform.

In addition, we need to straighten up the market places, especially in the setting of prices.

STUDENT (*from Beijing Normal College*): A lot of students have asked for an improvement in the system of education. The Central Committee admitted that one of the fundamental failures in the ten years of reform lies in the neglect of education.

HE DONGCHANG: Last April, the State Council established an educational exploration group on the authority of the Central Committee.

STUDENT: (*from Beijing Science and Technology University*): When we were demonstrating near Tiananmen on April 27, we saw huge numbers of soldiers. We didn't understand why. It may be necessary to have police on the spot to assure order, but troops are a sore sight to the people. Please explain this.

YUAN MU: I mentioned this earlier in responding to the question put forward by a student from the Chinese University of Politics and Law. The Beijing government set up ten regulations regarding demonstrations in the capital area. Our purpose is to protect social order, to protect the interest of the majority, but not to defend a particular individual's interest. Everybody must observe the demonstration laws. We did not approve of your pouring into the streets without applying for a permit. There you were, so we sent out the police. But Beijing does not have enough police to handle that kind of situation, so we asked the army to help. We did not approve of that demonstration because it violated the law. The government had to do something to express its disapproval. We sent out police first, but the police could not stop the

students because they thought they were confronting their own brothers and sisters. If we did not show our opposition to the protest, anybody in Beijing might follow your example and find excuses to take to the streets at any time.

Our orders to the policemen before they went to their posts was that no violence would be allowed no matter what happened. That was our biggest concern. We were not so worried about the police line being broken by you. I wonder if you knew that after the student demonstrators left the Square, about several hundred people gathered and made a scene. We must rely on the police to handle a riot like that. What else could we do to maintain order in Beijing? Same with campus order. I hope you people will understand the police and the government. Our laws are not perfect. The demonstration law is an example. It is not yet finalized; we need to make it better. You and I do not have too many differences on this point. I am not sure if I have answered all your questions. I can only say this: we must protect the sanctity of law.

STUDENT (*from Central Institute of Nationalities*): May I ask Comrade Yuan Mu a question? I am a Party member. When Comrade Hu Yaobang resigned, the Central Committee did not give any explanations of his resignation. At the memorial service, Comrade Zhao Ziyang praised him in a eulogy filled with nice-sounding words. My question is that since Comrade Hu Yaobang made so many contributions, as the eulogy said, to our country's reform, why should the Central Committee let him go without a word? Wasn't he the general secretary of the Party?

YUAN MU: I want to explain first that because I am a spokesman for the State Council, I do not intend to respond to questions relating to the Party. But I am a Party member, so let me tell you what I know. Comrade Yaobang was a great proletarian revolutionary and a great politician. He dedicated his life to the Party and to socialism; his contributions were great. Everyone wanted to honor him. I don't like the word, nice-sounding. Let's drop it. His resignation early in 1987 was in the way of self-criticism for the mistakes he had made. It was he who felt himself no longer suitable for the general secretary's office. His offer to resign was

accepted by the political bureau. Then the seventh meeting of the Twelfth Congress of the Central Committee discussed his proposal and passed it. I found everything concerning his resignation normal. There was nothing wrong with it. That's my personal opinion.
STUDENT *(from Beijing Institute of Nationalities): I don't believe in such a thing as a perfect man. Comrade Hu Yaobang made some*

mistakes in his life. But it had to be a terrible blunder to put him out of office. Why, then, was nothing mentioned in the memorial speech?
HE DONGCHANG: *I'd like to remind you of two sentences toward the end of the speech. "Hu Yaobang stood firm in defending truth; he was brave in admitting his mistakes and correcting them." You may have overlooked that.*

The death of Hu Yaobang triggers the student movement, and the failure of the CCP to deal with the movement results in bigger demonstrations.

April 30, Sunday

The Shanghai Municipal Committee of the CCP decides to "overhaul and consolidate" the *World Economic Herald* and to send a group to oversee the paper's work since Qin Benli, the dismissed editor-in-chief, has been insisting on his stand and the staff members of the paper have been resisting the instruction from the Propaganda Ministry of the Municipal Party Committee. This development brings about much criticism from journalists and intellectuals in Shanghai and Beijing, and lots of supporting telegrams are sent to Qin Benli. In Beijing, 150 journalists of the *People's Daily* ask the top leaders of the paper to engage in a dialogue with them about the *Herald* incident.

At the invitation of Beijing Municipal Government, twenty-nine students from sixteen Beijing colleges talk to Party Secretary Li Ximimg and Mayor Chen Xitong on the topic of official profiteering. At the students' request, the two leaders make known their personal total incomes on the spot to show their freedom from corruption.

The Central Academy of Fine Arts in Beijing holds a photo exhibition at which 250 photographs of the recent student movement are displayed. Some photographs of police beating up students at the Xinhuamen Gate on April 20 have been taken away by the authorities. All the works are displayed without captions since, the sponsor students explain, "the photographs can stand alone as evidence indicating the student movement does not violate the Constitution and law."

Student leaders, including Chairman of the FBSU Wuer Kaixi and Standing Committee member Wang Dan, hide out temporarily because it is rumored the authorities will secretly arrest student leaders.

The banner "The People's Police Love the People" moves the policeman. (A photo from the exhibit)

An exhibition of photos of the activities of mourning over Hu's death is held.

Well-known intellectuals Yu Haochen (right) and Li Honglin visit the photo exhibition.

Zhao Ziyang and his grandson.

May 1, Monday

The Hong Kong College Student Union convenes and decides to establish the Chinese Democracy Foundation to raise money and to plan a mass gathering and demonstration for May 4.

May 2, Tuesday

Ten thousand students from East China Normal University, Fudan University, and other colleges in Shanghai march on the main streets in Shanghai and gather in the People's Square, protesting the Municipal Party Committee's actions against the *Economic Herald*, shouting "Restore Qin Benli's position," "Journalism should tell the truth," "Down with special privileges," and "We want democracy." The parade is kept in order by the organizers. After the march, many students stage a sit-down demonstration in front of the municipal government building.

In France, overseas Chinese writers and artists establish the Temporary Committee for the Chinese Democratic System. Yadin, the famous author of the novel *Red Sorghum*, heads the organization. The establishing declaration says: "Only democracy and freedom can rescue China from its deep crisis," and "Without democracy, China will become the deadweight of the world."

The FBSU sends a petition to Zhongnanhai, headquarters of the Central Committee and the State Council, demanding a dialogue.

May 3, Wednesday

Efforts should be made to encourage young people to demonstrate their potential, to appreciate their own value, and to develop their character, says Zhao Ziyang at a meeting commemorating the seventieth anniversary of the May Fourth Movement. The meeting is held in the Great Hall of the People, and three thousand young people are present. Zhao Ziyang, general secretary of the CCP, addresses the meeting and tells the students that the demands of students and other people for promoting democracy, combating corruption, and developing education and science correspond with the aims of the Party. Zhao encourages young people, by displaying the spirit of patriotism, democracy, and science, to combine personal responsibility with the destiny of the nation, the individual's role with the collective, and great ideals with actual conditions. But he also urges them to maintain stability, for if social unrest returns with large-scale social conflict and disruption of production, study, and work, "a country of promise will be turned into a country of hopelessness and turbulence."

State Council spokesman Yuan Mu, Vice-Minister of the State Education Commission He Dongchang, Party Vice-Secretary of Beijing Municipal Committee Wang Jiamiao, and Vice-Mayor Yuan Liben hold a press conference. Yuan Mu says that the U.S.-based "reactionary organization

Alliance for Democracy" is a "black hand" behind the student movement. Yuan also says that for years someone has been filling students' minds with misleading ideas, establishing illegal ties on campuses, but "they should not think that the authorities do not know of their activities," Yuan warns. Yuan Mu accuses Fang Lizhi, the well-known dissenter, of suggesting that the Western countries should hold the recognition of human rights as a precondition of their investment in China. "History," he says, "will judge the conspiratorial role Fang Lizhi plays in the disturbance."

In Hong Kong, fourteen organizations respond to the FBSU's "Letter to the Hong Kong People," holding a joint news conference and appealing to the Chinese government to hold a dialogue with the college student representatives. They also call on the Hong Kong people to closely follow the democratic movement in mainland China and to donate money to support the student movement. The fourteen organizations include the Teachers' Association, the Federation of Unions, the Christian Workers' Association, the Federation of Social Workers, and the Educational Action Organization.

May 4, Thursday
A Hundred Thousand Students Demonstrate and Deliver the "New May Fourth Declaration"

In Beijing, a hundred thousand students from fifty-two Beijing colleges and more than thirty major colleges of other parts of the country start their demonstrations at eight A.M., marching from their campuses to Tiananmen Square. The march goes much more smoothly than that of April 27, with only one confrontation at Xidan (west of Tiananmen Square) with a police line that is quickly broken. Citizens cheer the students and bring food and drink to them all along the street. At one P.M. parades from each school meet in Tiananmen Square; with parades from other sections of the society, an estimated two hundred thousand people

gather there, shouting "We want dialogue, not scolding," "Equal dialogue, not idle talk," "Down with censorship," "Support the *Economic Herald*," "Not chaos, not the Cultural Revolution," and slogans satirizing Yuan Mu and He Dongchang's dialogue with students. FBSU leaders address the gathering and say again that widespread official corruption has to be dealt with before the four modernizations can be achieved. They insist that the student movement is not against the government, but patriotic by nature. The FBSU releases "The New May Fourth Declaration," calling for the establishment of democracy first on campuses,

Five hundred journalists in Beijing participate in the May 4 demonstration. Their banner says, "We want to tell the truth; don't force us to lie."

and eventually in the whole society. The gathering ends at four in the afternoon.

Five hundred journalists from the Beijing-based mass media join the students in an unprecedented protest calling for press freedom. The journalists, from Xinhua (New China News Agency), the *People's Daily*, Zhongxin (China News Service), the *Guangming Daily China News*, the *Science and Technology News Daily*, the *Asian Pacific Economic Times*, the *Workers' Daily*, and the *Peasants' Daily*, brandish signs reading, "We want to get the facts out," "Don't force us to lie," and "People have the right to know."

Mass demonstrations sweep the country. In Shanghai, tens of thousands of students

Journalists parade. The banners say: "News belongs to the people" and "Open journalism."

take to the streets to protest censorship. In Nanjing, the capital city of Jiangsu Province, several thousands demonstrate in front of the provincial government building, demanding a dialogue with provincial leaders. In Hangzhou, the capital city of Zhejiang Province, about five thousand march in the streets, shouting "Down with corrupted leadership" and "Support Qin Benli"; they attract thousands of onlookers and supporters. In Guangzhou, several thousand students take to the streets demanding that special privileges be abolished and the maligning of intellectuals be stopped. In Changsha, the provincial capital of Hunan, at least six thousand students and one thousand workers march together; their streamer reads, "End the rule of the old men." This is the first time the students have been joined by workers; police armed with electric clubs take positions along the streets, but no clashes are reported. In Wuhan, the provincial city of Hubei, tens of thousands of students from twenty Wuhan-based colleges stage a demonstration in the center of the city, shouting "Work for democracy, fight for freedom." In Xian, four thousand students march in the main street of the city, shouting "Long live Democracy." In Fuzhou, the capital of Fujian province, three thou-

sand students parade through the streets, and some three hundred demonstrate in front of the provincial government building, requesting a dialogue. In Chunqing, the capital city of Sichuan Province, two thousand students hold a May Fourth march. Police open the way for them and maintain order.

Chinese students abroad continue to support the democratic movement. Chinese students rally on the streets of Chicago, Houston, Hawaii, Ottawa, London, and Paris to show their support of democracy and freedom in China. Chinese students in the United States and Canada form the Alliance of Students from the People's Republic of China.

Five thousand students from fourteen colleges in Hong Kong and Macao, including the East Asian University in Macao, rally at Charter Garden in the central district of Hong Kong to support the movement. Some forty thousand Hong Kong dollars raised at the meeting will go to the Chinese Democracy Foundation. The Hong Kong Students' Union expects to meet Xi Jiatun, head of the Xinhua Hong Kong branch, and to forward a statement in support of the student movement next week.

Journalists parade. The banner says, "We want to speak but can't."

May 4 demonstration is a gathering of unprecedented size, made up of students, teachers, cultural workers, etc.

The recent demonstrations do not indicate political instability in China, Zhao Ziyang, general secretary of the CCP, tells governors of the Asian Development Bank, then in its twenty-second annual meeting in Beijing. When talking about domestic issues, Zhao insists that the demonstrators mean in no way to oppose the fundamental

The procession comes through Tiananmen Square.

Students in Beijing working in concert with students in Shanghai demand, "Give us back the Economic Herald.*"*

system of China, but to correct operational errors in the Party and the government, that this is reflected by the slogans of the demonstrations, such as "Support the Communist Party," "Support socialism," and "Support the Constitution and reform." Therefore, the leader says, there will be no major disturbances in China; the Party will give direction to the students' concerns and eventually sweep out corruption. The prac-

tices with which the students and other people are dissatisfied, Zhao says, stem from "imperfections in the socialist legal system and democratic supervision" and from "lack of openness of the operation," which gives rise to rumors and exaggerations. In order to exchange views, promote mutual understanding, and explore the settlement of issues of public concern, the general secretary urges that extensive consulta-

Boycott classes but not studies.

Raising money.

tions and dialogues be pursued with students, workers, intellectuals, non-Communist parties, and prominent citizens from all walks of life.

The *People's Daily* publishes an editorial entitled "Carry Forward the May Fourth Spirit, Promote the Causes of Reform and Modernization." The tone of the editorial is mild in comparison with the one on April 26. In this historical turning point of social transformation, young people are seen now as a vital new force.

Strikers resume class after the mass rally. Zhou Yongjun, a member of the FBSU's Standing Committee, announces at the end of the mass rally in Tiananmen Square that the two-week-long class boycott will end today. The decision has been made by the representatives from fifty-two colleges. However, Zhou reiterates the FBSU's demand for a dialogue with the government and says that the Federation will continue to negotiate with the government about the dialogue.

May 5, Friday

Most Beijing colleges resume class, but not Beijing University and the Beijing Normal University. Meanwhile, the FBSU keeps trying to get government recognition of their organization and continues to publish the *News Report*.

The FBSU dialogue delegation continues to pursue a dialogue with the government, listing as topics for discussion: 1) matters of every sort arising from the massive student movement, including the April 26 editorial of the *People's Daily*; 2) how to advance reform; and 3) how the government is to guarantee the human rights that are written into the thirty-fifth item of the constitution. The students demand also that the dialogue be televised live and be reported truthfully.

Premier Li Peng says that the aims of the government and those of the students are the same. Although the government disapproves of "some actions of some students," many of the students' demands are in line with the aims of the government, Li says at a meeting with heads of delegations to the twenty-second annual meeting of the Asian Development Bank and other ADB officials. "I can tell you," he says, "that the political situation in China is stable," and assures his audience that the government will strive to safeguard national stability and simultaneously to "earnestly overcome its shortcomings and reduce corruption."

Indictments are drafted on behalf of the *Economic Herald*. Heads of the civil-law and administrative-law teaching and research sections of the China University of Political Science and Law draft three indictments complaining that Jiang Zemin, Party secretary of the Shanghai Municipal Committee, tarnished the reputation of Qin Benli, the chief editor of the *Herald*. Jiang Zemin, addressing a meeting of ten thousand Party members and cadres in Shanghai, says that the report of the forum in Hu Yaobang's memory printed in the April 24 issue of the *Herald* would aggravate the situation.

The Economic Herald *incident in Shanghai reaches its climax in early May; a group of lawyers has drawn up a letter to sue Jiang Zemin, the mayor of Shanghai.*

May 6, Saturday

The FBSU delegates hand in a petition to the department in charge of people's representations to the general office of the CCP Central Committee and the State Council. It is addressed to the CCP Central Committee, the NPC Standing Committee, and the State Council and requests that leaders send officials to meet the students as soon as possible so that they can plan the dialogue. The student representatives expect to receive an answer at the same department on Monday afternoon.

May 7, Sunday

The FBSU delegates receive a notice from the general office of the Central Committee and the State Council informing them to come by the department the next day for the response to their petition. The head of the FBSU dialogue delegation says that if their petition is turned down, they will consider the reasons given but will not abandon the pursuit of a dialogue.

Students split over whether to resume class. In spite of the FBSU's decision to return to the classroom, students at Beijing University decide after a vote to continue the strike.

The *Economic Herald* is sealed up for the second time, for printing a statement by the Chinese Association of World Economics denouncing the Shanghai Party Committee's decision to remove Qin Benli from office, as not conforming to the laws of appointment and removal of officials. Several Shanghai lawyers form a legal group and are prepared to bring charges against the Party secretary if he persists in attacking the *Herald* for publishing the statement.

May 8, Monday

The government has not decided if it will hold direct dialogues with the students, the FBSU delegates learn at the department in charge of people's representations to the general office of the CCP Central Committee and the State Council. The students are informed that the Party and government officials prefer to have broad contacts and dialogues with workers, peasants, intellectuals, students, teachers, and people with non-party affiliations. The students will hear more about their petition on Thursday, an official of the department says.

The Beida Preparatory Committee decides to stage a limited class boycott to support the FBSU's efforts toward dialogue. The Committee puts forward five demands as conditions for ending the class boycott: 1) that the *People's Daily* apologize for its April 26 editorial and give the student movement fair and objective treatment; 2) that the government recognize the autonomous student unions; 3) that the State Council make known at once the statistics on *guandao* cases and set up an office to investigate and fix blame for official profiteering; 4) that the

Beijing journalists gather at Lu Xun Museum, to discuss support for the Economic Herald.

Shanghai Party Committee annul its decision and allow Qin Benli to return to his office; and 5) that the Beijing Municipal Government revise the ten rules of demonstration law.

General Secretary Zhao Ziyang speaks on issues raised by the student movement, saying that "The situation has not become acute because the Party and government have all along adopted a very tolerant and restrained attitude, and because most students have acted with increasing reason." He says that many of the demands voiced by the students are the same issues that the Party and government are striving to resolve. Zhao Ziyang believes that the solution to those problems will be found through democratic and lawful procedure and that this will help strengthen the country's democratic and legal underpinnings.

The young Beijing scholars insist that politics has much to do with economy, especially in the period of systematic economic adjustment; and that if the problem of *guandao* is not solved, reform will not be able to continue. A doctoral candidate at the People's University points out that in the past years Party discipline has been getting loose and corruption has been widespread among the bureaucrats, and that this is one of the main causes for the people's loss of identification with the government. A young scholar from Beijing University says that to put the economy in order means not only watching expenses but also cleaning up corruption in the government; therefore, the government's failure to sweep out corruption causes the difficulties in the economic adjustment.

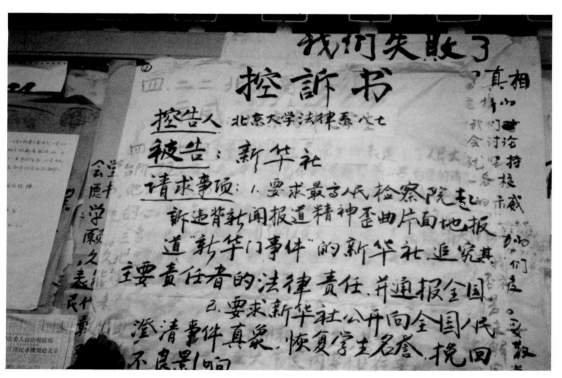

In early May, law students of Beida try to sue the New China News Agency.

May 9, Tuesday

A petition signed by a thousand Beijing journalists is presented to the secretariat of the All-China Journalists Association, demanding a dialogue on press reform with leading officials in charge of the media in the Party's Central Committee. Hu Qili, a member of the CCP Politburo Standing Committee who is in charge of the press, expresses approval of the petition. The petition raises problems as topics of the dialogue: 1) the *Economic Herald* incident in which Qin Benli was dismissed as editor-in-chief of the newspaper; 2) the news coverage of the students' activities in the past weeks, which was far from enough and not objective, a failure of the news media caused by censorship and in violation of the principle set down by the Thirteenth National Congress of the CCP that impor-

tant events should be made known to the people; 3) State Council spokesman Yuan Mu's statement during his dialogue with the students in Beijing on April 29 that "news reporting in China is based on a system of chief editors being in charge of everything in their units," which does not conform to the facts. When the petition is handed in, some thousand students from six colleges in Beijing gather outside of the association building in support of the journalists. They chant "The Internationale" and shout "Journalists, don't be afraid, demand democracy and report the facts," "Support the *Economic Herald*," and "Long live Qin Benli." The students later march to Tiananmen Square and stop at the gate of the *People's Daily* before their return to school.

The banner says, "Open journalism," May 9.

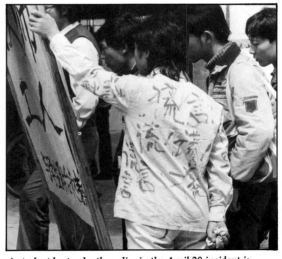

A student beaten by the police in the April 20 incident is angry. The words on his back say, "Lies, lies, lies."

May 10, Wednesday

Thousands of students from more than ten Beijing-based colleges including Beijing University, Qinghua University, and Beijing University of Aviation and Aeronautics ride their bicycles in a demonstration in Beijing, demanding freedom of the press. This is the largest demonstration of the week in Beijing. Some of the students put pieces of cloth on their heads bearing the slogan, "We are willing to die for freedom." They shout "The media should tell the truth" and distribute leaflets announcing that

"Bureaucrats use the State treasury as their own, destroy the country's economy, and cause terrible inflation. Is this not turmoil? They don't think so!" Other leaflets rebuke the bureaucrats for impeding political reform, repressing intellectuals, and letting public security deteriorate. At two P.M., the students march to the building of the Central People's Radio Station, shouting "freedom of press," "fight censorship," "support the journalists," "support the *Economic Herald*," "*People's Daily* lies to the people," and "reform, *People's Daily*!" At about three P.M. the demonstrators stop at Xinhua News Agency, chanting "Xinhua News, telling the truth." At about four P.M. the students on their bicycles stop at the building of the Propaganda Department of the CCP Central

May 9. More than a thousand Beida students stage a bike demonstration in support of the journalists demanding "open journalism."

Committee, shouting "censorship no, press freedom yes," and then ride to the *People's Daily*. Police do not intervene but try to maintain order and keep the streets open to traffic.

The back door of Zhongnanhai, Xinhuamen, is also heavily guarded.

Journalists demonstrate.

Writers and editors demand freedom of the press.

53

More than forty Beijing writers stage a two-hour demonstration, carrying a banner reading "Chinese writers, the conscience of the nation," shouting "freedom of the press," "freedom for all media," and chanting "The Internationale" as they march. Each of the writers present wears a white T-shirt reading, on the back, "poets, the voice of freedom" with a large character meaning *human*, and the writer's name and titles of his works on the front. The writers' procession starts at the West-Straight Gate of the city and moves through Tiananmen Square along with the students' procession.

Zhao Ziyang (left) and Li Peng at the First Plenary Session of the Thirteenth Central Committee of the CCP, 1989.

May 11, Thursday

Students decide to hold mass demonstrations and to invite Soviet leader Gorbachev to address them on the campus of Beijing University when he comes to China on an official visit on May 15. To support the Beijing students and to participate in the planned demonstration, five hundred students of Nankai University in the nearby city Tianjin have come to Beijing by bicycle, and a group of Shanghai students from Fudan University is on the way to Beijing. An official tells the FBSU students by telephone that the Central Committee is still considering the students' requests for a dialogue.

The enlarged Politburo of the CCP meets in Beijing to consider the request for dialogue and to seek a solution to the problem of the student movement. The top leader, Deng Xiaoping, does not attend the meeting. Some senior officials, in charge of propaganda and the united front (the CCP's effort to unite non-Party people to work along with the Party), write to the Party's top leaders urging them to enter into dialogue with the students as soon as possible, asking that some of the top leaders, including Zhao Ziyang and Li Peng, take part, rather than officials like Yuan Mu, who could only fuel the fire.

May 12, Friday

The *People's Daily* calls on the students to resume class. The editorial is mild, quoting Deng Xiaoping as saying to the president of Iran: "China is also striving for a stable international and domestic environment in which to work for development." The editorial urges the students to calm down and to consider what Zhao Ziyang said, that attitudes of calm, reason, restraint, and order should prevail and that problems should be approached in a democratic and lawful manner.

State Council spokesman Yuan Mu holds a press conference at the All-China Journalists' Association and expresses his belief that students "will consider the political and social stability of our country" and "the reputation of our socialist country in the world." He also says that there is no plan to launch a major campaign against bourgeois liberalization.

The Dialogue Preparatory Group of the Central Committee is established. Headed by Rui Xinwen, member of the Secretariat of the CCP Central Committee, the group is to hold a dialogue with Beijing journalists. Members of the group include Wang Renzhi, head of the Propaganda Department of the Central Committee; Du Daozheng, minister of the State Press Ministry; and Yang Yi, member of the Secretariat of the All-China Journalists' Association. At the same time, Hu Qili, member of the Politburo Standing Committee of the CCP Central Committee, briefs heads of the Beijing media to make them ready for dialogue, while journalists from thirty-two Beijing-based media, who signed the petition on May 9, also make preparations for the meeting.

May 13, Saturday

Gathering at the Beijing Normal University and led by FBSU chairman Wuer Kaixi, two thousand Beijing students march to Tiananmen Square where they begin a hunger strike to demand the dialogue, requesting that it be televised live. Students from Beijing University announce a "Fasting Declaration" and take an oath to stay with it until they achieve their goal. The writers' seminar in Beida gives a banner to the hunger strikers at their departure for the Square reading "You warriors are expected to return victorious." The students arrive in Tiananmen Square at four P.M. and sit at the base of the Monument to People's Heroes, with headbands that say "fasting" and coats that say "Without democracy, we would rather die." Some twenty thousand supporters surround the hunger strikers.

General Secretary Zhao Ziyang calls on the students to consider the honor and interests of the country and to be reasonable during Soviet leader Gorbachev's visit. The Party chief also says, to the Beijing workers' representative, that the issues raised by the students and workers will be placed on the agenda at the mid-July Plenary Session of the NPC Standing Committee.

The "Last Lunch"; teachers entertain their students before the latter begin the hunger strike.

Declaration of Hunger Strike

In these bright and beautiful days of May, we are beginning a hunger strike. We are young, but we are ready to give up our lives. We cherish life, we do not want to die.

But this nation is in a critical state. It suffers from skyrocketing inflation, growing crime rates, guandao and other forms of bureaucratic corruption everywhere, concentration of power in a few people's hands, and the loss of a large number of intellectuals who would now rather stay overseas. At this life-and-death moment of the nation's fate, countrymen, please listen to us!

China is our motherland.

We are the people.

The government should be our government.

Who should speak out, if we should not? Who should act, if we should not?

Although our bones are still forming, although we are too young for death, we are ready to leave you. We must go; we are answering the call of Chinese history.

Our honest feelings of patriotism and loyalty to the nation were distorted as "turmoil," and we were accused of being the tools of a "handful" who have "ulterior motives."

We ask of every Chinese citizen—every worker, peasant, soldier, civilian, celebrity, every government official, policeman, and our accusers—that you place your hand on your heart and ask yourself: What wrong have we done? What "turmoil" have we created? What causes have led us to protest, to demonstrate, to boycott classes, to fast, to hide ourselves? Why did this happen? Our words were not heard in good faith. We were beaten by police when we marched, hungry for truth. Our representatives knelt for hours, presenting our petition, only to be ignored by the government. Our request for dialogue has been put off again and again. The safety of our student leaders is now uncertain.

What shall we do?

Democracy is supposed to be the highest of human aspirations; freedom a sacred human right, granted at birth. Today these must be bought with our lives.

We will defy death to win life for the nation.

But we know that we are still children, the children of China. Mother China, look at your children. We do not want to die. We want to live and live fully; we are coming into our best years. We want to learn more, for China is poor. We do not want to end our lives when China is still backward. But if the death of one of us, or several, can make many lives better, we have no right to hold onto our lives.

We say to our dear mothers and fathers, do not feel sorry for us when we are hungry. To our uncles and aunts, do not feel sad when we leave this life. We have one wish, that the lives of everyone we leave be better. We have one request, that you remember this: our pursuit is life, not death. Democracy is not a task for a few; it takes generations.

When a horse is dying, his cries are awful. The words of a dying person are kind.

Goodbye, friends, take care! The living and the dead must be faithful to one another.

Farewell my love, take care! I do not want to leave you now, but I must.

Farewell, father and mother, forgive us that we're being unfaithful as your children; we must be faithful first to our country.

Farewell, countrymen, please let us take this way to tell of our loyalty and love.

May this declaration, written with our lives, break up the clouds that cast their shadows on the People's Republic of China.

These are the reasons we are doing this:

1. to protest the government's indifference to the student demonstrations;

2. to protest the government's failure to

enter into a dialogue with students;

3. to protest the government's unfair characterization of the student democratic movement as "turmoil" and the further distortion of it in newspaper coverage.

Our requests are these:

1. an immediate dialogue between the government and the students on substantial and concrete topics with equal status;

2. an acknowledgment by the government of the legitimacy of the student democratic movement.

Time of the hunger strike:
   beginning at 2:00 P.M., May 13, 1989
Place of the hunger strike:
   Tiananmen Square
We are not creating turmoil. But there must be recognition of the student movement! And immediate dialogue, with no more delay! Because we believe there is no alternative, we are fasting for the people. We ask the support of all the democratic forces in China. And the press of all the world, we ask your support.

   The hunger strike volunteers
   from the universities and
   colleges in Beijing

May 14, Sunday

The second day of the hunger strike: At two o'clock in the morning, Li Tieying, minister of the State Education Commission, and Chen Xitong, the mayor, go to Tiananmen Square to meet with the students. They promise that a dialogue will be held and persuade the students to consider the country's image abroad. Supporting students carry banners and posters to the Square and stay overnight with the hunger strikers. Because it is Sunday, the number of bystanders swells to thirty thousand. The striking students shout new slogans: "I like the taste of rice, but I love the taste of democracy," "Dialogue, we want dialogue," "Without sincerity, everything is nonsense." And they sing "The Internationale." The first night of the strike is chilly, but the next day is sunny, so warm that more than ten strikers faint. Some of them are sent to the hospital.

The government decides to hold a dialogue with the students immediately. At four o'clock this afternoon, more than thirty students including the FBSU delegates Wuer Kaixi and Wang Dan meet with high-ranking Party and government officials at the United Front Department of the CCP. Representing the Party and the State Council are Yan Mingfu, member of the Secretariat of the CCP Central Committee and minister of the United Front Department, and Li Tieying, minister of the State Education Commission. The students strongly condemn the April 26 editorial of the *People's Daily* and demand official denial of its charge that the students were creating turmoil. Yan Mingfu expresses regret that the dialogue has not taken place earlier, but says it is impossible to disclaim the editorial at this time. He hopes that the students will take the larger situation into account. The students are disappointed, but they promise not to organize demonstrations on May 15. At 7:15 in the evening, there is an argument about whether the dialogue will be televised and broadcast on the spot, and the meeting is adjourned. Accusing the authorities of a lack of sincerity, the students then return to the Square and demand a dialogue directly with Zhao Ziyang and Li Peng.

The Beijing Public Security Bureau orders a cordon on Tiananmen Square from 8:30 A.M. to 8:30 P.M. of May 15 because of Gorbachev's arrival. The bureau orders the students and everyone else to leave the Square.

Two hundred and eighty-three Beida faculty members send a memorandum to the

A hunger striker tries to conserve energy in the chilly night.

Central Committee, the NPC Standing Committee, and the State Council on the matter of the fasting students. The memorandum calls for the government to: 1) hold a real dialogue as soon as possible; 2) deal honestly with the student movement as a whole; and 3) pay special attention to the petition coming from the hunger strikers and to the students' health. Some faculty say that if the government does not promise to hold a dialogue with the students they will also strike, beginning tomorrow.

Twelve noted scholars, including Yan Jiaqi, Wen Yuankai, and Yu Haochen, go to the United Front Department at 8:10 P.M. and sign a "Letter to the Students" to persuade them to see the larger picture and to withdraw from the Square.

Artists paint pictures to support the hunger strikers. "The people are with you."

Posters on the Monument in support of the democratic movement..

Student movements spread across the country. In Hanan, the far southern province of China, the movement forces Governor Liu Xuqin to hold a dialogue with students. In Jiangsu province, Governor Wu Guanzheng meets with a hundred journalists in a public forum. Two representatives of the Hong Kong Students' Union bring 140,000 Hong Kong dollars to Beijing to support the hunger strikers.

Hearing that the water supply on Tiananmen Square has been cut off, an old man brings water to the hunger strikers on his pedicab.

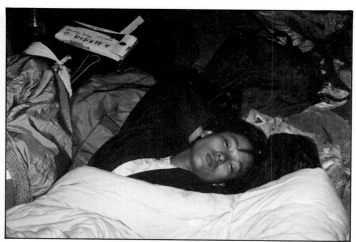

Common citizens send quilts to the hunger strikers.

Two hunger strikers share a cup of water.

61

May 15, Monday

The third day: After fifty hours of fasting, 130 of the 2,000 hunger strikers are exhausted and are sent to the hospital. The authorities have maintained the cordon around the Square but have not taken action against the striking students. From eight in the morning until noon, families of the students and teachers of more than ten Beijing universities arrive at the Square to support the hunger strikers. At one point, as many as eight thousand people crowd the Square; noticeable among them are students from the Chinese Youth Political Academy and a great number of college faculty.

A group of Chinese intellectuals, including such well-known figures as Yan Jiaqi, a political scientist, Bao Zunxin, a philosopher, and Dai Qin, a newswoman, along

Beginning May 15, more than twenty Hong Kong college students stage a sit-down demonstration outside of the New China News Agency, Hong Kong branch, and put slogans on the wall.

Students demonstrate at night to support the hunger strike.

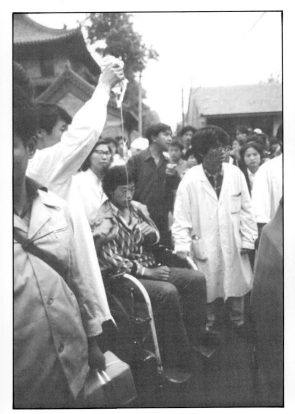

Medical workers put exhausted student in wheelchair.

An ambulance comes to the Square.

Medical workers are busy day and night saving the lives of hunger strikers.

with journalists from *Science and Technology News* and the *People's Daily*, and researchers from the Chinese Academy of Social Sciences, march into Tiananmen Square to support the hunger strikers. People cheer to them as they parade in, and police make no effort to enforce the cordon.

On their way to the Square, more than thirty of the intellectuals, including Yan Jiaqi, Liu Zaifu, a literary critic, Su Shaozhi, a political scientist, Dai Qin, and Lao Gui, a writer, announce the "May Fifteenth Statement" in support of the students. The main points of the Statement are that the government should not use force to repress the student movements, should recognize the legitimacy of the autonomous student unions, and should go on to reform the whole political system, and that the official media should not hide the facts of the student movement from the people or characterize the movements as turmoil and should admit that no one behind the scenes incited the movement.

Students on Tiananmen Square welcome Gorbachev. The poster says, "Salute to the ambassador of democracy."

From nine A.M. until noon, a dialogue continues between Li Tieying and Yan Mingfu and student representatives from twenty-two colleges. Li Tieying, member of the Politburo of the Central Committee and minister of the State Education Commission, says that the social conflicts brought about by the reform movement have brought about the present upheaval on the nation's campuses. Yan Mingfu insists that the mainstream of the students is patriotic and positive, but that the dignity of the country has been hurt by students' actions, and expresses the hope that the students will be reasonable so that their movement can be justified.

Yang Shangkun, state president, exchanges opinions with Soviet leader Gorbachev. Because the students have been occupying Tiananmen Square, the ceremony to welcome Gorbachev has to be held at Beijing airport. In a later meeting with Gorbachev, Yang Shangkun, state president, says that the reform has been going too fast and that this causes errors in policy making. The reform, he says, has to slow down.

About two dozen Hong Kong college students begin a hunger strike at the door of Xinhua Hong Kong branch, promising to stay with it as long as the students maintain their hunger strike in Beijing. Some eighty supporting students sit with them and hand over a "Fasting Statement" to Xinhua News Agency, expressing their disappointment in the condescending attitude shown by Beijing authorities in their talks with the students, and calling for restraint in dealing with the movement.

May 16, Tuesday

The fourth day of the hunger strike: More than three thousand students are involved, and six hundred of them have become exhausted from disease and hypoglycemia, and are hospitalized. But all the students have sworn to persist. Ten students from the Central Academy of Fine Arts declare a water fast to protest the authorities' decision to "peacefully resist the movement by not holding a real dialogue with the students." The first sixty hunger strikers who fainted rejoin the strike on their return from the hospital. Meanwhile, teachers from six universities, including Beida, join the students. There are also some workers among the strikers.

Support for the fasting students has spread through every segment of the population. Students from Beijing Second High School, Ninth High School, and 107th High School take to the streets, carrying a banner reading "You may fall, but we are coming." Hundreds of journalists from CCTV and the *People's Daily* hold a streamer asking people to stand strong against the April 26 editorial as they take to streets in an attempt to wipe out the shame of the newspaper. Workers from the All-China Federation of Trade Unions Beijing Steel Plant and China Heavy Machinery Tool Factory march to Tiananmen Square shouting "Workers with the students." Teachers from Shaanxi, Guizhou, Guangxi, and Hobei come to the Square, with a banner reading "Teachers from eleven provinces" and shouting support for the students. Other posters read "We're through with the politics of old men," and "If he can't talk to the people, the Premier had better step down."

At 5:25 P.M. Yan Mingfu, member of the CCP Central Committee Secretariat, comes to the Square alone and tries to persuade the students to stop the hunger strike. He expresses his understanding of the students' requests and tells them that he has communicated their grievances to the top leaders of the Party. He asks the students to be patient and to protect their health. He even indicates that he is willing to be a hostage to sit-in with the students in the Square. After a discussion among the student representatives, however, Yan's suggestions are rejected and the hunger strike continues.

Zhao welcomes Gorbachev.

General Secretary Zhao Ziyang says in his meeting with Mikhail Gorbachev that senior leader Deng Xiaoping is still China's helmsman, that this was decided at the First Plenary Session of the Thirteenth Central Committee of the CCP. Thus for the first time Deng's role in the Party is made clear. On the other hand, Premier Li Peng says to Gorbachev that the capitalist countries have no monopoly on freedom, democracy, and human rights, and that China will improve

in these areas as the political reform goes on.

Presidents of ten Beijing colleges, including Qinghua, Beida, Beijing Normal, Political Science and Law, and the People's University, release a statement in support of the students, warning that the fast is reaching its limit and that only a dialogue between authorities and students as equals can prevent a crisis. Hundreds of Beida professors form a "League to Support the

Beijing Students" and release a "Letter to the Nation," criticizing the authorities and demanding that the government hold a dialogue, not repress the student movement, and not persecute leaders of the movement in the future. Some Beida faculty go to Tiananmen Square to join the students.

The declaration of the Beijing students in support of their fast triggers campus upheavals throughout the country and in Hong Kong as well. Students in Shanghai, Zhejiang, Hubei, Hainan, Jiangsu, Sichuan , Shenzhen, and Hong Kong pour into the streets in support of the Beijing students,

staging sit-ins before the provincial and municipal government buildings. The hunger strikers in Hong Kong, gathered in front of the Xinhua building, vow not to give up their fasting if the Beijing hunger strikers do not give up theirs.

In Taiwan, the Kuomintang Central Committee releases an announcement expressing support for the students and saying that the mass pro-freedom and pro-democracy movement in mainland China during the past month are the results of the bankruptcy of Marxist-Leninist thought and the Communist system.

Near Tiananmen Square, citizens are reading the special posters about the hunger strike.

Red Cross ambulances park near the Square to rescue hunger strikers.

Some hunger strikers.

The skirt of a student hunger striker is covered with signs.

The slogan says, "The hunger strike has lasted one hundred and twenty-one hours."

Workers come to see the striking students.

After May 17, the situation becomes more radical. One poster says, "Step down, last emperor."

Student representatives from Hong Kong University and the Chinese University of Hong Kong demonstrate in Tiananmen Square.

Party members of CCTV demand, "Expel Li Peng from the party."

A political joke that means: "Yuan Mu is a fool," or "Yuan Mu fools the people."

May 17, Wednesday
Two Million March in Beijing

General Secretary Zhao Ziyang reads a written statement on behalf of all members of the Standing Committee of the CCP Politburo at two o'clock in the morning. He affirms the students' patriotic spirit in calling for democracy and law, but hopes that they will "exercise calm, reason, restraint, order, and take the interests of the whole country into account." The Party chief promises that the Party and government will definitely not square accounts "after the autumn harvest." Zhao appeals to the students to end the hunger strike. The students reject the plea and continue fasting.

The fifth day of the hunger strike: More than two thousand strikers have been sent to the hospital, and six are critically ill. The students have become very weak after a hundred hours, and many have produced complications; doctors say that their lives are in danger. It is hot today and may be cold tonight because the weather broadcast says that there will be thunderstorms tomorrow. The doctors are afraid that the students' conditions will worsen and disease could break out among them. At the temporary headquarters of the hunger petition group, students begin to work in relays.

The largest demonstration since the founding of the People's Republic takes place in Beijing. Two million people from all walks of life take to the streets spontaneously in support of the students' action for democracy, carrying streamers reading "Xiaoping Xiaoping, not good with his brain; he had better step down, and go sit at the bridge table"; "How are you Xiaoping, what a fool you are Xiaoping"; "Li Peng step down." The demonstrators include factory workers, peasants, intellectuals, journalists, and government office workers of the Foreign Ministry, the Propaganda Department of the CCP Central Committee, the United Front Department of the Central Committee, the State Systematic Reform Commission, and the State Education Commission. Also, more than a thousand officers of the People's Liberation Army join the massive march. Some thousand students arrive at the Xinhuamen Gate in the morning, shouting "Come out Li Peng," "Li Peng step down" and brandishing a banner reading "Turtle draws in its head." They stay for an hour and then return to Tiananmen Square.

Fei Xiaotong, vice-head of the NPC Standing Committee and chairman of the China Democratic League, says that he handed in an urgent petition to the Central Committee of the CCP suggesting an emergency meeting of the NPC Standing Committee to consider the student demands, but that the appeal was denied by the Central Committee.

More hundreds of thousands of students and others take to the streets to support Beijing students in twenty cities including Shanghai, Nanjing, Guangzhou, Shenzhen, Fuzhou, Xiamen, Guilin, Hangzhou, Tianjin, Wuhan, Qingdao, Haerbin, Changchun, Shengyang, Chendu, Chongqing, and cities in Shaanxi province and Xinjiang Autonomous District. In Hong Kong, students and supporting citizens hold rallies while various organizations send telegrams to the Central Committee of the CCP to show their support for the students.

The May Seventeenth Declaration: The well-known intellectuals Yan Jiaqi, Bao Zunxin, Li Nanyou, and a fourth person release a declaration blaming the long hunger strike on the Central Committee's indifference to the students' just requests. The document declares that "there is still an Emperor in China, only without the title," and that the student movement depends for its legitimacy on the judgment of the people, not the government.

Various individuals and organizations appeal to the students to end their hunger strike and ask that the Party and government leaders hold a dialogue with the students as soon as possible. Appeals come from the China Federation of Literary and Art Circles, All-China Women's Federation, presidents of eight colleges, and Chen Rong, a writer.

In the United States, Chinese students publish open letters in support of their fellow students in China. From several campuses in San Francisco they write General Secretary Zhao Ziyang and Premier Li Peng an open letter, appealing to them to hold a dialogue with the students immediately. Similar support is voiced at Cornell, Columbia, and other campuses in the New York area.

The poster reads, "Looking for Deng Xiaoping." Deng disappeared after his meeting with Gorbachev.

Customs staff in demonstration.

Workers of the Foreign Ministry in demonstration.

The poster says, "Under heaven denounce Li," which means, "The people all over China denounce Li Peng."

Cartoons of Deng and Li.

The words on the poster say, "Mourning the death of Deng and Li," implying the two should step down.

The couplet says, "The flower of freedom will never fade; the tide of democracy will never recede."

This poster put up by PLA men praises the democratic movement.

Demonstrations in Shenzhen.

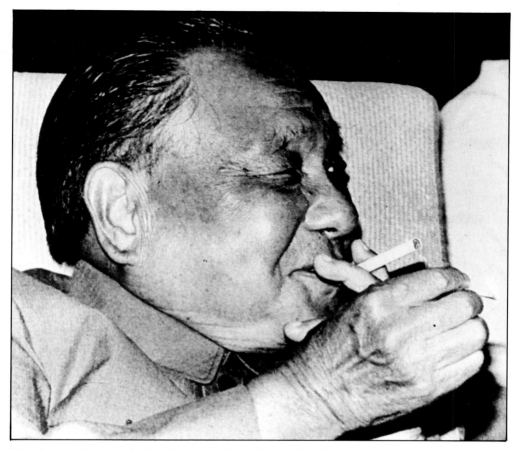

When demonstrations spread all over the country, Deng disappears from the stage.

"May 17 Declaration"
by Yan Jiaqi, Bao Zhengxin, Li Nanyou, etc.

Since two P.M. May 16, three thousand students have joined in a hunger strike that has now lasted one hundred hours. Seven hundred victims have fainted in the Square. This is a tragic event that never happened before in Chinese history. What the students requested is the retraction of the April 26 People's Daily editorial and the live broadcast of the dialogue between the students and the government. In spite of the fact that one after another the hunger strikers are falling down, and because the students' just demands failed to be treated with sincerity and attention, the hunger strike is continuing. Now the problem of China is exposed fully in front of the country and the whole world. That is, the dictator has unlimited power; the government has failed its responsibilities. It

is no longer human. Such a government is not a republican government, but a monarchy subject to a dictator.

The Qin dynasty has been gone for seventy-six years. But today China is still ruled by an aging emperor, although he does not wear the crown. Yesterday afternoon, general secretary Zhao Ziyang openly informed us that, in China today, any important issues have to stop at this old dictator. If he does not approve, nobody can negate the April 26 editorial. The students have fasted for nearly one hundred hours, and we do not have another choice. The Chinese people should not wait any more for the dictators to do self-criticism. We must rely on ourselves, on the people. Here, we want to declare to the whole of China and the world that the students' hunger strike has achieved victory. The students have told the world with their actions that the student movement is not "turmoil" but a patriotic campaign of democracy to bury the last dictator and monarchy.

Let us hail the victory of the hunger strike!
Long live the spirit of nonviolent petition!
Down with the dictatorship!
All dictators will come to no good end!
Retract the April 26 editorial!
End the old man government!
The dictator must resign!
Long live university students!
Long live the people!
Long live democracy!
Long live liberty!

Li Peng at the meeting with student representatives, May 18.

May 18, Thursday

At around five o'clock in the morning, members of the Standing Committee of the Political Bureau of the Central Committee Zhao Ziyang, Li Peng, Qiao Shi, and Hu Qili go to the Beijing Xiehe hospital to visit students exhausted from hunger. At the same time, Li Tieying, minister of the State Education Commission, visits the students in another hospital. Those who are visited insist that they initiated the movement not to overthrow the Chinese Communist Party but to urge the Party and the government to clean up corruption and to carry out political reform, and so regain people's confidence. The students ask the leaders to go to Tiananmen Square to visit the hunger strikers there. All four leaders agree that the students' requests are consistent with the government's policy and offer their wishes for the students' good health.

The meeting between Premier Li Peng and the students breaks up in discord. From eleven A.M. to twelve P.M., Premier Li Peng and other high-ranking officials, including Yan Mingfu and Li Tieying, both members of the Standing Committee of the Political Bureau, meet about a dozen student representatives, including Wuer Kaixi and Wang Dan, members of the unauthorized autonomous student union. At the outset, Li

Wuer Kaixi, student leader and hunger striker. After the meeting with Li Peng, he faints.

Peng says that he wants to talk about only one topic, how to rescue and guarantee the lives of the hunger strikers. Wuer Kaixi, interrupting Li Peng, asks that they go directly into the "substantive problems." Wang Dan makes two requests: 1) that the government acknowledge the student movement as a patriotic action, not disorder, and officially disclaim the April 26 editorial; 2) that

Zhao Ziyang visits exhausted hunger strikers in hospital, May 18.

it begin a dialogue immediately and televise the talks on the spot. Xiong Yan, another student representative, expresses his confidence that history will look upon this event as a democratic movement, and that to ask for the confirmation of the government is to find out "if the government is our own government." The authorities should be honest about the movement, he adds, and not be so concerned about face-saving. On the government side, Li Tieying and Yan Mingfu express concerns about the students' health, while Li Peng and Chen Xitong point out that demonstrations and campus upheavals have brought disorder in Beijing and have spread across the country. Not answering the students directly, Li Peng says that the "substantive problem," the first priority, is to save the lives of the hunger strikers, so all of the fasting students should be removed to hospitals immediately. The party and the government, he insists, have never indicated that the students were creating chaos, but he claims that the citizens' demonstrations are not in support of the hunger strike. Li Peng repeats his demand that the stu-

dents stop the fast, while ignoring the students' demands. The student representatives are disappointed, and the meeting ends on a bad note.

By the sixth day of the hunger strike more than two thousand fasting students have been hospitalized. Thirty students are now on the water fast that was started fifty-nine hours ago by the ten art students. All of the hunger strikers are in bad condition; some have not urinated for twenty-four hours, and others are suffering from circulatory problems. Doctors warn that this could cause permanent damage. Some of the fasting students catch cold, and doctors worry that a flu could break out. Hospitals and clinics go on overtime to treat the strikers, and ambulances shuttle back and forth on "the lifeline." In the meantime, the Beijing Red Cross organizes seventy buses to park in the Square to help shield the students from the elements.

Two million people demonstrate in the rain in support of the strikers. Beijing is half-paralyzed by the demonstration. Factory workers, students, and shop assistants walk together as the rain falls. Workers from some twenty important industries, including Heave Electrical Machinery Plant, Hoist Plant, Construction Machinery Factory, and Beijing Steel Plant carry banners reading "The workers are coming," "Forget our bonus," and "We are not afraid to be fired." Public security policemen in uniform drive three trucks on the streets to show their support. Other banners say "Rise and fall three times, step down again" (referring to Deng Xiaoping's political career), "We don't need a helmsman," and "No more life-long offices." The demonstrators hold Mao's and Zhou Enlai's portraits and ask, "Li Peng, do you think Premier Zhou would act like you if he were alive?" (Zhou Enlai was Li Peng's foster father.)

At six in the morning in Tiananmen Square an open letter from some PLA officers is read through loudspeakers. The let-

During the six days of the hunger strike, more than two thousand hunger strikers faint and are hospitalized.

ter asks that 1) force never be adopted to deal with the students; 2) dialogue take place at once; 3) military surgeons be sent to treat the students; and 4) the leadership of the army set examples in promoting reform.

Party members at Shenzhen University urge Deng Xiaoping to retire. The University's president, vice-president, and other Party members send a telegram to the Central Committee and General Secretary Zhao Ziyang expressing surprise that there is indeed a helmsman above the Party, saying that this is not in accord with the Party constitution. The telegram also points out that the Central Committee has made mistakes in coping with the current student movements and demands that the Politburo and the Secretariat of the Central Committee exercise authority as called for by the constitution. They follow this up by

The judges demonstrate, supporting the hunger strikers.

Workers support the students.

Medical workers say that the government has the "bureaucratic cancer."

initiating a petition from the citizens of the city; more than twenty thousand people sign it.

Members of the NPC Standing Committee and the Chinese People's Political Consultative Conference (CPPCC) appeal for an emergency meeting, affirming the hunger petition as a patriotic action, asking the Party and the government to hold a dialogue with the students immediately, expressing the hope that the fasting students will end their hunger strike, and calling for an emergency meeting of the National People's Congress. The appeal is signed by twelve members of the Standing Committee of the NPC, including Ye Duzheng, Feng Zhijun, Jiang Ping, Tao Dayong, Peng Qinguian, and Chu Zhuang, and eleven members of the CPPCC, including the famous painters Li Keran, We Guanzhong, and Huang Miaozi.

The Rescue Group of Chinese Cultural and Academic Circles is several widely esteemed intellectuals, including Xu Liangying, Yu Haochen, Yan Jiaqi, Gao Ao, and some others. The group blames Li Peng for creating disorder and calls for the students to resume eating, saying that their purpose—to arouse the people—has been achieved.

Throughout Guangdong, in cities such as Guangxhou, Shenzhen, Zhuhai, and Shantou, students demonstrate and raise money on the streets. College students in Shenzhen establish the autonomous student union, and more than a hundred students start a hunger strike in support of the Beijing students. In Shanghai, besides the students' demonstration, well-known writers and dissenters, including Wang Rowang, Bai Hua, and Dai Houying, form a "Shanghai Writers' Support Group" and march to show their support. More than two hundred students are also on a hunger strike in Shanghai, where about a dozen faint from hunger and are sent to the hospital. In Hanan Island and also in Guilin, in Guangxi province, tens of thousands of people take to the streets. In Tianjin there is a general class boycott, and nearly a hundred thousand students leave for Beijing to petition for democracy. In Chengdu, there is city-wide demonstration, with 550 students on a hunger strike. Student representatives have tried to hold a dialogue with the municipal government, but failed.

Students from high school and primary school come to support their big sisters and brothers.

Members of the Association of Fellow Students from Taiwan in Beijing hold a poster saying, "Save the children."

Students of Quhu Normal University come to Beijing.

The Dialogue between Li Peng and the Students
May 18, 1989 (Edited)

LI PENG: *Let's first focus on one subject, that is, how to make the student hunger strikers stop fasting. The Party and government are very concerned about the students' health. . . . You are all young—twenty-two or twenty-three at most. My own children are older than you. I declare that none of my children is involved in guandao. . . .*

WUER KAIXI: *Time is running out quickly. We're sitting here comfortably while our fellow students are starving outside, so please pardon me for interrupting. You said just now that we should focus on only one subject. We're not here because you invited us, but because of the hundreds and thousands of students in the Square who invited you to talk to us. We must decide the number of topics, not you. Fortunately we share some ideas, so let's focus on one subject, that is, the many students who have fainted from fasting. I think the question is not what problems to solve, but how to solve them. Our fellow students haven't returned to school yet. I'm sure that you know what that means.*

WANG DAN: *To end the hunger strike, the government should first meet our demands. Several million people are demonstrating to support the*

students. *Their actions show that they're on the students' side. We hope the government will listen to the people and solve the problems.*

WUER KAIXI: *It's very clear that the question is not how to persuade us who are present here to leave the Square. I'd like to state that, first, we know better than anyone else that the students need to leave as soon as possible. Second, it won't help if all of us at this meeting are persuaded because we consist only of one tenth of a percent of the students in the Square. It's not a matter of subordination to the majority. I believe if there is one single student who decides not to leave, the rest will keep him company.*

WANG DAN: *This isn't an opportunity to convince us, but to respond to our requirements. First, the government must acknowledge that the current student campaign is patriotic in nature, not "troublesome" as it was called in the April 26 editorial. Second, dialogues must start as soon as possible. If you can give us a satisfactory response to our demands, we'd like to return to the Square and do our best to persuade our fellow students to go back to school.*

WUER KAIXI: *Let me say again . . . First, the student movement must be given positive recog-*

nition and the April 26 editorial must be declared wrong. Up till now, nobody had said anything positive about the student movement. Everyone must come to understand the nature of the movement. It helps to know what it means in practice. There are several ways to do this. First, Comrade Li Peng or Comrade Zhao Ziyang should give a speech in the Square. It should then be followed by a speech at the Great Hall of the People, but I'm not sure whether that would be accepted. Another way is to use the People's Daily editorial. I wonder if the April 26 editorial was the product of a conference. If it was, I sincerely request an apology by the newspaper in the form of an editorial admitting that the article was a mistake. It must also admit the far-reaching significance of the student movement.

Dialogue means immediate, open, equal, direct, and sincere conversation with the true representatives of the students. The State Council has repeatedly said that dialogues aren't necessary. Now, as a representative of the thousands of students in the Square, I say again: it is necessary to have dialogues. What we're looking for is a meeting between the policy makers and the student leaders we select. This is also what we mean by equality.

XIONG YAN (student representative from Beijing University): I'm one of the representatives for the hunger strikers. . . . Although the government refuses to admit the significance of the great pro-democratic movement, it will gain its position in history. We want recognition from the government because we want to know whether it is still our government. . . . We should fight for communism. . . . We are human beings with conscience. We should cast away any selfish concern about losing face so that we can reach a solution. In fact, if the government admits its mistake, it will regain people's support. We're dissatisfied with you not because we're against you personally but because you're the premier.

You yourself admitted a moment ago that you started tackling the problem too late.

WANG ZHIXIN (student from the University of Politics and Law): I think there are a few things that need to be cleared up. One is that this is not simply a student movement, but a pro-democratic movement of all the people. Since May 13 more and more people have joined us. The stu-

dents can't control a situation like this, and we should not be responsible for it. I want to ask the government why, on April 22—after long hours of our kneeling in petition and our crying out a thousand times for our government leaders—didn't any of you people come out to see us? The hunger strike has lasted for seven days now, since May 13. According to international practice, a government, even one as bad as South Africa, has to respond on the seventh day. I hope China, a great country led by the Communist Party, can live up to expectations. Another aspect of the demonstration is the different age groups of the participants: we have kindergarten children, old men and women, people ranging from little kids to eighty-year-olds. Kids shouted: Drink some water, big sisters! Eat something! I wonder what the government thinks of them.

A STUDENT: I'm under the impression that several leaders agree that the students are not making trouble but upholding a meaningful movement; they were all nodding their heads. The students are actually carrying out a democratic campaign and exercising their constitutional rights. It's not just patriotic passion. People driven by passion will do anything, even if it's illegal. Our movement is one of poise, order, reason, and lawfulness.

SHAO GANG (student from Beijing University): None of us wants to make the situation more serious than it is. We know that China's progress lies in her stability, but the composition of the student movement has changed as more and more other elements join the demonstration. It may end up in a nation-wide campaign. Although the Central Party and the government recognize that the student movement is restrained, we can't guarantee that a nation-wide campaign would display the same restraint. Therefore, I urge you to accept our demands and prevent things from getting worse.

LI TIEYING (head of the national education committee): . . . We in the education committee have a lot of experience in setting up different kinds of channels to listen to the faculty and students. I don't want to see the student movement remain at the present level. It is in fact a national event; its demands have gone beyond educational areas. There are more political demands, and the situation is still developing.

If you ask me my opinion of the student

movement, . . . I would say that the students have demonstrated their patriotism through their criticisms, suggestions, and proposals. But many of their decisions aren't in line with our thinking. I think history is the best judge of this movement.

The movement could become inconsistent with the students' initial ideas. Both of us are against turmoil. Nothing will ever get done if there isn't a stable environment in China.

YAN MINGFU: . . . I'm confident that we'll find a resolution to the problem. Right now we need to send those who are very weak to the hospital. I suggest we reach an agreement on this. We must resolve the two problems separately.

As I said in a conversation with Wuer Kaixi and Wang Dan on the thirteenth of the month, things have gone far beyond what people can control. At that time, I raised three points. First, the students should leave the Square immediately and the hunger strikers should be persuaded to receive hospital treatment. Second, the Central Committee has authorized me to assure the students that they will be safe after they return to school. That was our response to the students' question about "squaring accounts after the autumn harvest." Third, if you do not trust me you can take us to your schools as hostages until the People's Congress begins its session. I was told that, after I left, Wang Dan and several other students presided at the meeting, and that some there agreed to my proposal but the majority did not.

Meanwhile the government and Party leaders made quite a few attempts to visit with the students at the Square, but because they could not get in touch with student headquarters, they were unable to enter the center. You may know of this already. More and more evidence shows that the three spontaneous student organizations are no longer able to influence the surging crowds. It's not likely that the crowds that keep pouring into the Square will listen to you. The direction this whole thing is going worries people. It seems the only thing that you can do is to persuade the hunger strikers to leave. Then we of the Central Committee and the government sincerely want to resolve the issues you students have brought up. An immediate problem is the safety of these kids. It concerns everybody. We must handle it with great care, as we want to be responsible to them.

CHEN XITONG: Comrades, you have all noticed what has happened in the last few days. Workers, peasants, intellectuals, and office workers are very worried about it. What kind of situation is this? A lot of people have called the municipal government and the Party committee requesting something be done through democratic and lawful channels, as Comrade Zhao Ziyang said. They also want us to stop the traffic confusion. Traffic is totally paralyzed these days. Although some workers have joined your demonstration in support of your petition, many more want to end the confusion. If the traffic problem gets any worse, the transportation of supplies for daily life will come to a halt. What that will mean to the life of the people and the country is clear to everybody.

Another concern of mine is the health of the hunger strikers. Paramedics and doctors from the Red Cross are doing their best to help them. A short whole ago they submitted a request to receive top priority in rescuing the hunger strikers, who are very weak now. They wanted us not to play with the students' lives, or to use them as bargaining chips. I want you to understand this too. We must guarantee the health of the hunger strikers. Fasting is unhealthy; it can even be deadly. After all, what's the point of suicide if there are other ways to resolve the problem?

LI PENG: Everybody's interested in discussing practical substantive questions. The first one I want to address is my proposal that the national Red Cross and the Beijing Red Cross be responsible for delivering the weak hunger strikers to hospitals immediately. I need support from Xiehe Hospital and from the students in the Square. In addition, I request all hospital personnel to give their utmost to nurse the student hunger strikers. Their lives should be made absolutely safe. No matter what differences we may have between us, the lives of the hunger strikers are our first priority. In this matter, the government has full responsibility. All the students in the Square should also be concerned with their comrades and lend a helping hand to the Red Cross.

I have directed all the big hospitals in Beijing to provide beds and all necessary medical facilities to treat these students.

The second question I want to address is that neither the government nor the Party has ever referred to the students as rioters. We have always emphasized the value of your patriotic enthusiasm. There were quite a few things you did right. Among the suggestions you made, I found that a lot are on the government's agenda and will be solved soon. One thing is certain, you people have taken a positive step toward pushing the government to get these things done in the future. We've wanted to do it for a long time, but there were too many obstacles in our way. Your sharp criticisms are helping the government tackle these difficulties; therefore, I consider your actions positive. However, things are not developing in accordance with your kind-hearted wishes, imaginations, and patriotic passion. Beijing is now in total disorder, and the confusion is spreading to the rest of the country. Yesterday in Wuhan, a key link in China's railroad system, the railway traffic was stopped for three hours. Crowds of people are flooding into Beijing. Some of them are students; others are jobless people disguised as students. Beijing is paralyzed. I'm not blaming Wuer Kaixi or Wang Dan for what has happened. The Chinese People's government is responsible for the people. We cannot ignore what's happening. We must protect the safety of the students, the factories, and our socialist society. . . . Chinese history has seen a lot of unexpected turbulence. The people didn't want upheavals, but things got out of control. The third point I want to make is that a lot of workers, civilians, office workers, and even some workers from the State Council have gone into the streets to support you. But please don't misunderstand their intentions. They're doing this to show their concern. They don't want you to destroy your health. It's all right if they send food and drink to you and ask you to take some. It's also all right for them to try to persuade you to leave the Square. However, I cannot approve of those who encourage you to continue the hunger strike, no matter what their motivation is. Being a responsible government, we must express our attitude . . . (someone interrupts). I haven't finished yet. We have agreed to speak one at a time.

. . . As the premier and as a Party member, I shouldn't hide my opinions. I will talk about this at a more appropriate time, not today. Now that I've finished what I wanted to say, I think it's pointless to be tangled up in this particular issue.

Before I close, let me appeal to everyone here. If you can't make the decision for them to stop fasting, carry my petition to them. I hope they'll stop the hunger strike and get medical care as soon as possible. I extend my sympathy and concern for them on behalf of the government and the Party. I hope they accept this simple but urgent request from the government.

WUER KAIXI: I want to remind you of something. You talked about "getting tangled up in the problem" a moment ago. What we want is to resolve the matter with a humanistic understanding. I'm going to repeat what I said earlier, but I want to stress one point, that is, certain leading comrades do not seem to understand that the key is to persuade not us but those hunger strikers in the Square to leave. I've told you clearly enough the conditions under which they will leave. There is only one possible outcome, that is, if only one hunger striker remains in the Square, the other thousand will probably stay with him. Then, regarding the Red Cross, I believe, I appeal to Premier Li and other government leaders to deal with the practical means of the rescue. We don't want to be tied up with it. This is also our opinion. Please accept our conditions. The students in the Square are fasting; if you don't respond immediately, we will consider the government insincere. Therefore, it is a waste of time for us to stay here any longer.

WANG DAN: Premier Li thinks there's disorder and bad influences in the streets. I can tell you that the government must take full responsibility for that.

XIONG YAN: Comrade Li mentioned disorder. I want to have three minutes to analyze the simple relationship between disorder and the student movement. When a society or country has upheavals, are they caused by student movements? My answer is no. In my opinion, when a country is unstable, something is definitely wrong with its social structure. Students take actions to try to pinpoint what is wrong so that the government may resolve the problem. Any attempt to suppress the student movement, or as we call it the democratic movement, will cause social upheaval. This is a very simple truth.

YAN MINGFU (reading from a slip of paper): The hunger strike headquarters wants its representatives to return immediately.

(*Wuer Kaixi faints and falls down while Yan Mingfu announces that the meeting is over. Several paramedics rush to his rescue.*)

YAN MINGFU: *Premier Li Peng has expressed the attitudes of the Party and the government. The first thing we must do now is the move the hunger strikers to hospitals for medical care. We'll leave the rest of the discussions for some other time.*

WANG ZHIXIN: *This wasn't a dialogue, but an introductory meeting.*

YAN MINGFU: *Yes, it was.*

Four A.M., May 19. Zhao Ziyang and Li Peng come to Tiananmen Square to visit the hunger strikers. Zhao says, "I am sorry," with tears in his eyes. Li says nothing.

May 19, Friday
Zhao Ziyang Visits Fasting Students in Tiananmen Square

At 4:45 in the morning, Zhao Ziyang and Li Peng, top leaders of the Party and the government, visit the fasting students in Tiananmen Square for the first time. "I am too late," says Zhao Ziyang with tears in his eyes. He appeals to the students to end the hunger strike. The issues they have raised will be resolved eventually, Zhao says, but things are complicated, and resolving the problems will be a long process. It is reported that Zhao speaks to the students with emotion, his hands trembling. Students cheer his speech and applaud. Li Peng does not speak. At nine in the evening, the students decide to end their hunger strike but to continue sit-ins in the Square. However, this is an unofficial visit, and reports say that senior leader Deng Xiaoping opposed it.

It is rumored that Zhao Ziyang proposes, in a meeting of the Standing Committee of the Politburo of the CCP Central Committee, to officially retract the April 26 editorial of the *People's Daily* and to sweep out *guandao* (profiteering). He suggests, the leak says, that the sweep start with his own son and Deng Xiaoping's son. Zhao's suggestion enrages Deng Xiaoping; Deng expresses that those who want to deny the April 26 editorial are dividing the Party. Then the seventeen committee members and Deng Xiaoping vote sixteen to two in support of a resolution that the student movements have been creating disturbance. Zhao Ziyang then presents his resignation to the Politburo.

Beijing factory workers spontaneously establish the Beijing Workers' Autonomous Trade Union in support of the student movements.

A Beijing newspaper, *Chinese Voice*, publishes a statement by more than a thousand intellectuals describing the student movements as patriotic and democratic activities. The writers and academics who signed the statement include famous writers Ba Jin, Ai Qing, Yan Jiaqi, Liu Zaifu, Su Shaozhi, Li Zehou, Wu Zuxiang, Ye Junjian, Li Honglin, Su Xiaokang, Wang Luxiang, and Wang Zengqi.

Four official institutions, the Chinese Economic System Reform Research Institute, the Agriculture Study Center, the International Research Institute of the Chinese Trust Company, and the Association of Young Economists, release a statement declaring their discontent with the way the government has been playing for time.

Mass demonstrations in support of the Beijing students take place throughout the country in places such as Shanghai, Tianjin, Shengyang, Hebei, Shandong, Guizhou, Heilongjiang, Guangzhou, Shenzhen, Zhuhai, Shantou, Meizhou, Zhaoqing, and Hanan Island. In Shanghai, a million people take to the streets.

Li Peng tells a special envoy of the prime minister of Australia that bringing an end to the turmoil is a purely domestic issue. He says that the disorder in Beijing has spread to other parts of the country. The government will take responsibility for ending the turmoil, but the process of reform and the open-door policy will be carried on without disturbance, the premier states.

May 20, Saturday
Li Peng Calls the Student Movement Turmoil

Li Peng addresses central- and municipal-level Party, government, and army cadres at a meeting held by the CCP Central Committee and the State Council in Beijing. Li says that the demonstrations and hunger strikes disturb the social order and create chaos. He demands that the students stop the demonstrations immediately. He claims that a handful of people are attempting to create turmoil in order to achieve selfish political goals and blames these few for the attacks against top leader Deng Xiaoping that occurred during the demonstrations.

Yang Shangkun, state president and vice-chairman of the Military Commission of the CCP, gives a speech after Li Peng's at the cadres' meeting. Yang announces that People's Liberation Army troops will enter and garrison Beijing. He stresses that the troops are not being sent to deal with the students, but to maintain order in the city. Zhao Ziyang does not show up at the meeting.

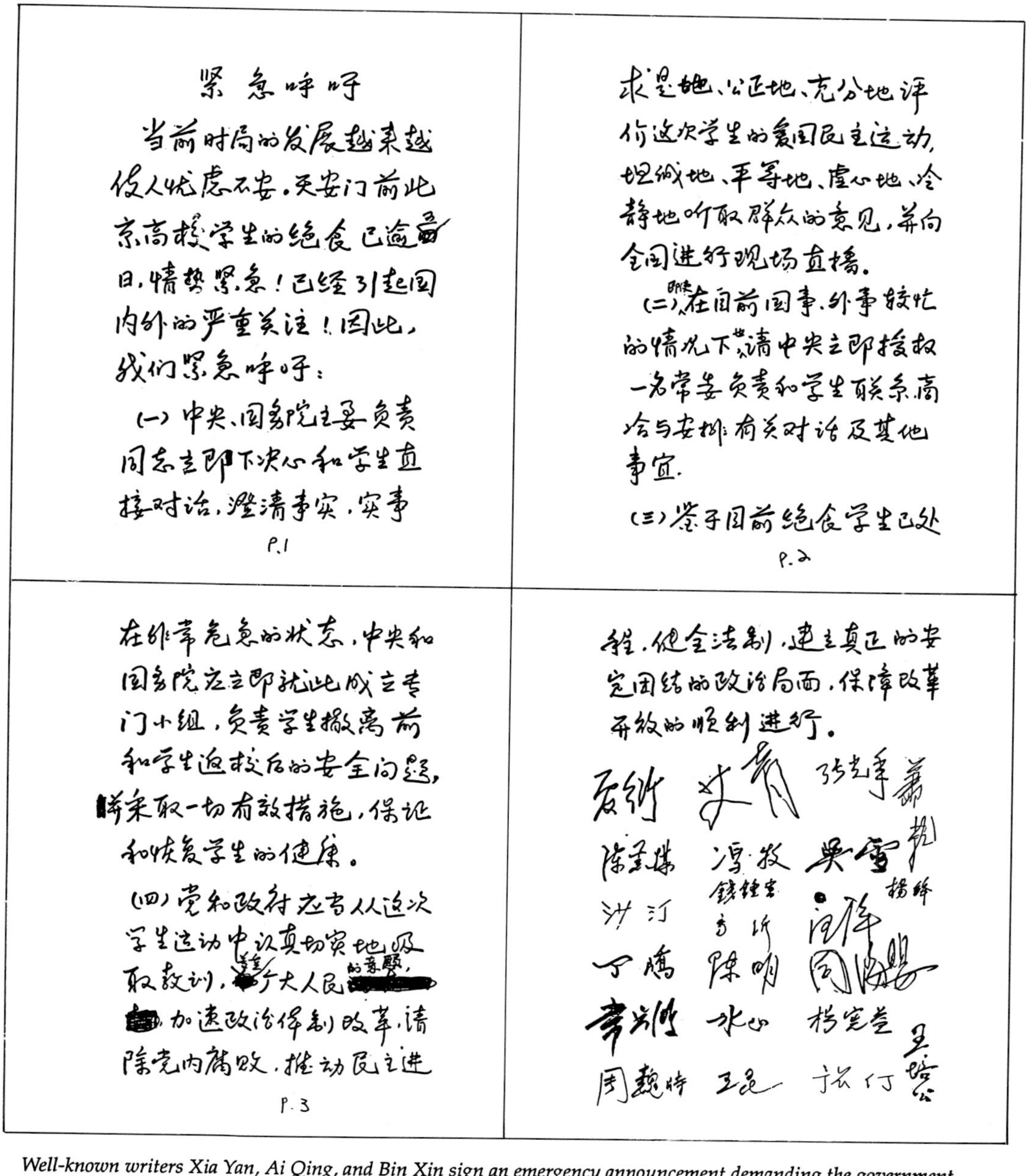

紧 急 呼 吁

当前时局的发展越来越使人忧虑不安。天安门前北京高校学生的绝食已逾四日，情势紧急！已经引起国内外的严重关注！因此，我们紧急呼吁：

（一）中央、国务院主要负责同志立即下决心和学生直接对话，澄清事实，实事

P.1

求是地、公正地、充分地评价这次学生的爱国民主运动，坦诚地、平等地、虚心地、冷静地听取群众的意见，并向全国进行现场直播。

（二）在目前国事、外事较忙的情况下，请中央立即授权一名常委负责和学生联系商冷与安排有关对话及其他事宜。

（三）鉴于目前绝食学生已处

P.2

在非常危急的状态，中央和国务院应立即就此成立专门小组，负责学生撤离前和学生退校后的安全问题，并采取一切有效措施，保证和恢复学生的健康。

（四）党和政府应言行一致认真切实地吸取教训，个大人民

加速政治体制改革，清除党内腐败，推动民主进

P.3

程，健全法制，建立真正的安定团结的政治局面，保障改革开放的顺利进行。

Well-known writers Xia Yan, Ai Qing, and Bin Xin sign an emergency announcement demanding the government open dialogue with the students immediately.

87

Yang Shangkun says the troops' movement into Beijing is not intended to repress students.

Li Peng gives the "important speech" at the general meeting of cadres of the party, government, and army in Beijing.

The CCTV announces that martial law is proclaimed by the national government.

Two hundred thousand students stage a hunger strike protesting Li Peng's speech. The students in the Square had decided the night before to end the hunger strike but to continue the sit-in. However, Li Peng's speech, which is broadcast in the Square, greatly disturbs the students. At 1:40 in the morning, after a meeting of representatives from every school, the FBSU declares a general hunger strike in Tiananmen Square. The decision receives thunderous applause from the two hundred thousand students in the Square. Students, still maintaining order, brandish banners, chant "The

Internationale," and shout "Long live the people," and "Long live freedom." While the students still insist on peaceful demonstration, thousands of citizens pour into the streets to obstruct the military vehicles heading to Tiananmen Square.

Premier Li Peng proclaims that, as of ten A.M., martial law is to be enforced in the Eastern, Western, Chongwen, Xuanwu, Shijingshan, Haidian, Fengtai, and Chaoyang districts of Beijing. Under martial law, demonstrations, petitions, class boycotts, work stoppages, and other mass activities that impede normal order are banned. In addition, common Chinese people and journalists from abroad as well as from Hong Kong, Macao, and Taiwan are banned from engaging in various activities to investigate and report news. These three Beijing Municipal Government orders are signed by Mayor Chen Xitong.

A great number of troops, escorted by armored cars and tanks, head to Tiananmen Square. In spite of the martial law declared by Li Peng, many citizens pour into the streets to stop the troops with trucks, buses, and human bodies as well, shouting "The people's army does not charge the people." At the western suburb of Beijing, citizens stop four thousand troops in one hundred military vehicles; northwest of Tiananmen Square, helmeted troops in thirty military trucks are surrounded.

Reportedly, the troops sent to Beijing were ordered a week ago not to read newspapers or watch television or listen to radio, and the only news they have been allowed to read is the April 26 editorial from the *People's Daily*. The soldiers and the lower-ranking officers knew nothing about the situation in Beijing or about their mission, it is rumored.

Chinese students demonstrate in Tokyo. Li Peng is characterized as a Nazi leader.

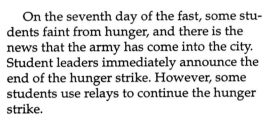

The slogan reads: "The people's patience is limited."

In the morning of May 20, two hundred thousand students on the Square declare a hunger strike.

On the seventh day of the fast, some students faint from hunger, and there is the news that the army has come into the city. Student leaders immediately announce the end of the hunger strike. However, some students use relays to continue the hunger strike.

At 5:08 A.M., the Beijing Workers' Autonomous Union calls for a general strike until the army is withdrawn. The strike will not include utility departments or postal and telegraph offices.

The student dialogue delegation sends a telegram to Wan Li, chairman of the NPC Standing Committee, calling for him to conclude his visit to North America and return to China immediately. The delegation asks Wan Li to summon the NPC Standing Committee and to exercise the highest authority allowed him by the Constitution. Should anyone use force to suppress the unarmed students, the delegation also declares that it will ask the Supreme Procuratorate to institute proceedings against him and will appeal to world opinion and the International Association of Human Rights.

Although the troops cannot enter the center of the city, some army officers in

plain clothes have reportedly sneaked into the city and taken over the Central Television Station, Central Radio Station, and the offices of the Central Committee of the CCP.

In the morning, people in Beijing begin to march in an orderly fashion to Tiananmen Square, disregarding martial law. The masses shout "Down with Deng Xiaoping! Down with Li Peng!" and hold banners that say "Government alienates the people; all walks of life are against it," and "Democracy, yes! Freedom, yes! Martial law, no! Dictatorship, no!" Among the demonstrators, about two dozen judges and police officers from the Chinese High-ranking Judges Training Center have been seen.

Foreign countries including Great Britain, the United States, and Thailand urge the Chinese government to exercise restraint in dealing with the students.

The Beijing students receive support both from other parts of the country and from outside the country. Demonstrations take place in Shanghai, Xian, Hunan, Chengdu, Wuhan, Shaanxi, Henan, Chongqing, Haerbin, Guangzhou, as well as in Hong Kong, Taiwan, Macao, and the U.S.

Beijing citizens stop the troops in the western suburbs of the city.

A cartoon in front of Xinhuamen.

A hundred thousand citizens try to stop the troops from coming into Tiananmen Square.

Beijing is seething. The banners say: "Oppose martial law" and "Convene the National People's Congress."

"Step down Li Peng."

The toy bear is named Li Peng.

The banner reads, "The Federation of Autonomous Workers' Union of Beijing."

Li Peng's Speech at the May 20 Meeting of Cadres from Party, Government, and Army Organs in Beijing

Comrades:

The Standing Committee of the Political Bureau of the Chinese Communist Party Central Committee has called this emergency meeting in order to mobilize all the cadres from the Party, government, and army organs of the central bureaus and the cadres from the local capital level. We must take resolute measures to put an end to the turmoil. We must restore social order and maintain stability so that we can ensure the smooth progress of reform, of the policy of openness, and of socialist modernization.

The briefing by the Beijing Municipal Party Committee secretary has shown that the capital is in a grave state of anarchy that is going from bad to worse. There have been many violations of the law and of discipline. The situation, which had seemed to calm down toward the end of April, is becoming more unstable as huge numbers of students and civilians are getting involved in demonstrations and many campuses have come to a standstill. Traffic is jammed everywhere, and Party and government offices have been attacked. The deterioration of public security is seriously interfering with the normal life of the city. As you all know, the Sino-Soviet summit conference, which was the focal point of the world, had to either reschedule its agenda or cancel some of the activities altogether. This severely hurt China's standing in the international community.

The hunger strike is still going on in Tiananmen Square. The students' health is deteriorating, and some of them are in imminent danger. In fact, the hunger strikers are being used as "hostages" by a few people trying to force the Party and the government to yield to their political demands. These people do not show a single sign of compassion. The Party and government have so far taken every possible action to provide medical treatment and first aid, and we have held several dialogues with student representatives and have sincerely expressed our desire to continue to listen to their opinions in the future. We had hoped that the students would stop fasting, but they have not. The student representatives admit that they are no longer able to control the situation; crowds keep pouring into the already packed Tiananmen

Square, shouting their own demagogic slogans. If we fail to end this chaos resolutely and immediately—if we go on tolerating it—it is very likely that we will end up in a situation that none of us would like to see.

The situation is becoming more grave. The turbulence has already spread to many other cities in the country. More and more people are demonstrating. In some places, they have attacked Party and government offices. Serious cases of beating, smashing, and looting have been reported from more than one place. Recently, it was reported that some rioters stopped trains on major tracks and paralyzed transportation in the national railway network. All of these things have shown us that if the situation isn't stabilized as quickly as possible a nationwide crisis will soon develop. Our open policy of reform and modernization is being severely threatened, and so are the fate and the future of the People's Republic.

The Party and the government have stated again and again that the majority of the students are kind and honest and did not mean to cause such turmoil. They are patriotic and prodemocratic; they want us to end corruption. In this respect, there is no difference between what they want and what the Party and government are striving to achieve. The questions and suggestions brought up by the students have exerted a positive influence on the Party and government already. But such activities as demonstration, protest, and class boycotts will damage social stability. They will not solve the problems but will rather cause a turn for the worse. The seriousness of the matter tells us that things in the Square are not developing the way the students intended.

It has become more and more clear that a very small handful of people are using the situation to reach their political goals, that is, to negate the leadership of the Party and the socialist system of China. They openly shout slogans saying that bourgeois liberalization must not be opposed. Their purpose is to obtain absolute freedom to wantonly attack the four cardinal principles. They spread rumors, smear Party leaders, and call the leaders names. They have now pointed their spearhead at Comrade Deng Xiaoping, who has made great contributions to our country. Their purpose is to overthrow the leadership of the Chinese Communist Party and the people's government that was lawfully elected by the National People's Congress, and to completely destroy the people's dictatorship. They stir up trouble, set up secret ties, organize various kinds of illegal associations, and try to force the government to recognize them. It is obvious that they are making preparations for opposition parties in China. If they should succeed, everything we have worked so hard to accomplish in reform and open policy, in democracy and law, and in socialist construction will all come to nothing. Chinese history will show this to be a time of great retrogression; the hopeful China will become a hopeless, futureless country.

We must be firm in exposing the handful's political conspiracy, so that we can differentiate between the majority of the students and those who want to stir up trouble. We are doing this out of our love and concern for our youths. It was out of that same concern that we adopted an extremely patient attitude in the past weeks. We did not want to hurt good people, especially not young students. Nevertheless, the handful who hid themselves behind the scenes plotting turmoil misinterpreted our good will as weakness and thought it an opportunity to take advantage of the Party. They spread rumors to confuse the people and escalated the turmoil. They have caused so much damage and confusion to the whole country that we must take resolute measures to stop it once and for all.

It must be stressed that even under such grave circumstances we must still be careful to not discourage the patriotic feelings of the young students and to differentiate them from the handful of plotters. We must not be too hard on the radical speeches they have made in the student movement. In addition, we will continue the dialogues between the Party and the government and the majority of the students, people of all walks of life, including those who have taken part in rallies, demonstrations, class boycotts, and hunger strikes. The dialogues will be held at several levels and through several different channels and may use diverse forms. If the students' demands are reasonable, we will respond actively and positively. For instance, we will listen attentively to suggestions and criticism in regard to ending corruption, guandao, and bureaucracy in order to improve the work of Party and government.

In the past few weeks, leaders, teachers, and students of many universities have done all they could to persuade the students from taking to the streets. They have also worked hard to maintain order on campus. Police officers and the armed police have made their contributions to maintaining order and public security. To office and factory workers and shop assistants who have stuck to their jobs and have done their utmost to keep life running normally, I want to extend heartfelt thanks on behalf of the Party and government. I think the people will always remember you for that.

In order to put an end to the turmoil and restore order, on behalf of the Party and the government, I call upon you all in this emergency to heed the following: 1) The students who are on hunger strike in Tiananmen Square today must please stop fasting, leave the place, receive treatment, and restore their health. 2) Students and other groups of people in the city must stop demonstrations of any kind. You must be compassionate and give the strikers no more so-called "voice support." Whatever your purpose is, the more "support" you give them, the further you push them into a blind alley.

Comrades! Today I also call upon the whole party, the whole army, and the whole nation to unite as one and take action, each from his assigned post, and to contribute to stopping the turmoil and restoring stability to the country.

All levels of Party organizations must unite the masses by carrying out more sophisticated political and ideological propaganda. You should demonstrate leadership and stand like a fortress in a battle.

All members of the Communist Party must strictly obey the Party's disciplines. You must not only stay away from any activity that may jeopardize unity and stability, but also work as a vanguard and a role model in eliminating the turmoil.

All government office workers must remain at their posts, be loyal to their duties, and maintain their daily working routine.

All the security police and armed police must make more efforts to restore traffic and social order. You must take more measures to strengthen public security by resolutely wiping out all illegal and criminal activities.

All manufacturing and commercial workers must maintain discipline in their work and remain at their posts.

Schools at all academic levels must maintain their normal routines. Those who are boycotting classes must return to school unconditionally.

Comrades! The Chinese Communist Party is a ruling party. Our government is a government for the people. To be responsible for our holy motherland, and for the people as a whole, we must take firm measures to end turmoil immediately so as to defend the Party's leadership and the socialist system. What we decide will surely receive the support of all Party members, all members of the Youth League, all the workers, peasants, and intellectuals, people of all walks of life, and members of all the Chinese democratic parties. It will also receive support from the People's Liberation Army, which is delegated by the Constitution the task of defending the country and the people. Meanwhile, we hope that the majority will give their full support to the PLA and the police in restoring order in Beijing.

Comrades!

While we are striving to maintain stability and unity, we must continue to carry out the four cardinal principles. We must persist in the open policy and reform, in reinforcement of democracy and law, and in eliminating corruption. Strive for the constant progress of the cause of socialist modernization!

Yang Shangkun's Speech to the Meeting of Cadres from the Party, the Government, and the Army (Condensed)

I fully support Li Peng's report and the orders he laid down on behalf of the Party and the government.

Recently in Beijing, all office routines, class schedules, traffic, and food supply have been interrupted. Such turmoil is by its nature a state of anarchy.

The Sino-Soviet summit conference was a historical event, but we were unable to hold the welcoming ceremony in Tiananmen Square as scheduled. It was held instead at the airport.

Several meetings were to be held in the Great Hall of the People, but we were forced to move them to the guest house at Diaoyutai, and we

A huge banner in front of Tiananmen Square demanding that the National Congress convene, Li Peng resign, Deng Xiaoping and Yang Shangkun retire.

had to cancel some programs. We could not carry out the scheduled ceremony in which Mr. Gorbachev was to present a wreath to the Monument of the People's Heroes. This made us look very bad in terms of our diplomatic relationships.

We did not even have the right of way today when we were rushing to this meeting. We had to leave an hour earlier than usual to get here on time. If we let this situation continue, the capital will not be a capital any more. The municipal government cannot function, nor can the State Council. This is an extremely grave situation.

For the sake of restoring order and defending public security, some of the PLA had to move to the outskirts of Beijing to maintain stability.

The armored carriers that you saw on your way here were the troops that have just arrived in Beijing.

We were forced by necessity to take this step. Beijing's police department was already power-less in the face of such a massive disturbance. The municipal armed police and their colleagues have been working overtime for almost a month. Many of them are sick from working long shifts, often around the clock. It has become commonplace for them to work two or three days on end. Therefore, we found it impossible not to ask the army for help in restoring order to the capital.

The appearance of the army on the outskirts of Beijing should by no means be seen as a way to handle the students. It is here to restore order to the capital and to protect the important departments and offices from being interrupted or attacked. We moved the troops in precisely for that purpose: to maintain order, not to suppress the students. You will see that I am right in the next few days.

I sincerely hope that you and all the businesses and trades in the country, including all the democratic parties in China, will understand and support this decision.

Martial Law Issued by Li Peng to Be Imposed in the Main Areas of Beijing
May 20, 1989

In view of the serious turmoil that has taken place in Beijing, which has greatly disturbed social order, security, and the people's normal life, and in order to extinguish the turmoil, to maintain the city's peace, to ensure the safety of the citizens and their properties, to protect public properties, and to guarantee that the daily routine of the central and municipal governments is not disturbed, the State Council hereby announces that, in accordance with the sixteenth regulation under item eighty-nine of the Constitution, martial law will be carried out in certain parts of Beijing beginning at ten o'clock Beijing time on the twentieth day of May, nineteen eighty-nine. The martial law will be imposed by the Beijing People's government, which is entitled to work out the details of these measures as necessary.

Premier of the State Council
Li Peng

Martial Orders by the Beijing People's Government
Order No. One

In accordance with the martial law issued for parts of Beijing by Li Peng from the State Council, the Beijing People's government hereby gives this order to end the social turmoil and restore order to production, education, research, and the capital's normal life:

1. Beginning ten A.M. May 20, 1989, the following districts will be under martial law: East City, West City, Chongwen, Xuewu, Shijingshan, Haidian, Fengtai, and Chaoyang.
2. During the period of martial law, no demonstration, petition, boycott of classes, strike, or any other form of action that will jeopardize public order is allowed.
3. Nobody is allowed to fabricate and spread rumors, to visit universities, to speak in public, to hand out leaflets, or to incite social unrest.
4. Attacking Party, government, or army offices is expressly prohibited. No one should interrupt work in radio stations, television stations, or communications buildings, or damage important public facilities. Absolutely no fighting, smashing, looting, burning, or other forms of destruction will be tolerated.
5. It is prohibited to disturb any foreign embassies or the United Nations offices.
6. During the period of martial law, security officers, armed policemen, and PLA soldiers have the right to employ any means, including the use of force, to stop a violator.

The citizens' observation of the above order is expected.

Mayor
Cheng Xitong

Martial Order by Beijing People's Government
Order No. Two

In accordance with the martial law issued by the State Council to be exercised over certain districts of Beijing, and in order to maintain order for the capital, Beijing People's government hereby announces this order:

1. All foreign nationals in Beijing must observe the martial orders announced by the Beijing People's government in accordance with the State Council's martial law command signed by Premier Li Peng.
2. No foreign personnel are allowed to enter an area where a violation of the law is being handled.
3. The officer on duty has the right to use all means to stop a violator.

Mayor
Cheng Xitong

The slogan on top of the bus says, "Oppose martial law."

Martial Order by Beijing People's Government
Order No. Three

During the period of martial law, correspondents must know the following regulations:

1. *No Chinese or foreign newspaper reporter is allowed to use interviews as ways to incite people, nor is he allowed to publish instigating reports.*
2. *Without special approval by the municipal government of Beijing, no foreign reporters or reporters from Hong Kong or Macao are allowed to interview, photograph, or to videotape in offices, organizations, schools, factories, mines, enterprises, or residential areas.*
3. *Our personnel on duty have the right to stop any violators on the spot.*

Mayor
Cheng Xitong

Reporters from Hong Kong, Macao, and western countries set up in Tiananmen Square.

May 21, Sunday
Zhao Ziyang Loses Power

Seven senior leaders of the army write to Deng Xiaoping, chairman of the Military Commission of the CCP, and the PLA martial law headquarters in Beijing asking that the army not enter the capital city. The seven leaders are Ye Fei, Zhang Aiping, Xiao Ke, Yang Dezhi, Chen Zaidao, Li Juqui, and a seventh man.

It is rumored that Zhao Ziyang has lost power and has been put under house arrest. At the meeting held on May 19, Zhao did not show up. The Xinhua news said that his absence was due to illness.

At three in the morning, about fifty PLA tanks arrive in Tong County, about nine miles from Beijing, and continue to head to Tiananmen Square. On the other side, fourteen military carriers full of soldiers reach Andinmen Gate, a little more than two miles from the Square; obstructed by the citizens, the troops withdraw to the Jing-Chang highway but try to take the subway to the Qianmen Gate. More than a million people crowd around Tiananmen Square in the early morning to bar the way of the troops. Twenty thousand workers and stu-

Student sit-down strikers confront the armed police, protesting the imposition of martial law.

dents from outside Beijing form a dare-to-die corps and commit to protecting the students in the Square. Several clashes have been reported, and it is said that one soldier and over forty civilians have been injured.

Students in Tiananmen Square vow to hold out to the end. It is rumored that the army will take final action soon, and the atmosphere in the Square grows tense. Students have gathered a large amount of water and cloth in case the army uses tear-gas grenades. However, order is still maintained in the Square, and the student leaders once again call for the students to persist in the principle that they should "not respond when berated, not strike back if beaten."

In the Square, students representing more than one hundred colleges present a "Letter to the Nation" in the evening, calling

Citizens in Beijing pour into the street to stop the troops and use buses to block the main thoroughfares.

on the Standing Committee to engage in a direct dialogue with the students in order to deal with the current crisis and the severe antagonism between the government and the students.

The PLA headquarters for the enforcement of martial law in Beijing declares a "Letter to Beijing Citizens," explaining that the army is there not to deal with the students but to maintain order for Beijing.

The official China News Service reports the situation on Beijing streets for the first time. According to its story, there are no traffic accidents, no beatings, no smashing, and no looting, and the food supply is normal. The report, however, conflicts with what is said in the "Letter to Beijing Citizens" from the martial law headquarters.

Fifteen noted academics including Yan Jiaqi, Pang Pu, and Jin Guantao issue a "Declaration in Defense of the Constitution," demanding an emergency NPC Standing Committee meeting be called to resolve the current crisis.

Five well-known intellectuals including Yan Jiaqi, Bao Zunxin, and Su Xiaokang

send a telegram to Wan Li, who is on an official visit to North America, calling for him to return immediately to resolve the crisis.

At around eleven A.M., the foreign TV stations are no longer able to use satellites to transfer news from Beijing, telephone lines are disconnected for a while, and radio transmissions are disturbed as well. Some foreign reporters have gotten in trouble during their interviews with common Chinese people.

The United States government once again calls for restraint on the part of the Chinese government.

The situation in Beijing concerns many people. Demonstrations take place in Beijing, Xian, Nanjing, Henan, Xiamen, Wuhan, Haerbin, Shanghai, Guangzhou, Chengdu, Changsha, and Xiangtan. In many foreign countries, such as the United States, Canada, Australia, Denmark, Sweden, France, the Soviet Union, and Japan, Chinese as well as natives stage demonstrations and sit-in protests in support of the students in China.

A million people march in Hong Kong to support the Beijing students. The processions start in the central district of the city, then march to the racecourse opposite the Xinhua Hong Kong branch to hold a big rally. At the rally, Xu Haining, a member of the Xinhua Hong Kong branch, speaks out in condemnation of the dictatorship of the Li Peng government.

A league of Hong Kong citizens in support of the Beijing democratic movement is formed at the mass rally.

The troops are surrounded.

Students from the Northeast organize a dare-to-die corps.

People hope that Wan Li, who is visiting North America, will convene the National Congress and dismiss Li Peng from office.

Taking a rest.

Students put steel tubes on the street.

More than one million people rally in Hong Kong to protest the movement of troops in Beijing.

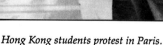
Hong Kong students protest in Paris.

Children can protest, too.

A Letter to the People of China by Student Representatives from the Universities and Colleges

Dear countrymen, dear parents who gave us birth and brought us up:

We, the students who represent the hundreds of universities and colleges of China, are writing you this declaration at Tiananmen Square.

In order to advance the cause of democracy in China, three thousand students began a hunger strike in the Square on May 13, 1989. We had some confidence in the government at that time, but that trust was lost during the seven days of fasting. At nine P.M., May 19, the hunger strike ended with the beginning of a sit-down strike. To our great dismay, the government not only continued to ignore our requests, but also declared martial law that same day, leading the country into a very grave crisis.

For two whole days and nights, students and civilians in Beijing made peaceful but strenuous efforts that proved martial law in Beijing to be impossible. We firmly support the bill put forward by several dozen members of the Standing Committee of the People's Congress for an emergency meeting. We appeal to the Standing Committee of the People's Congress, the highest official body in China, for a direct dialogue in regard to the repeal of martial law and the withdrawal of troops from Beijing. We also want to discuss the conclusion of the class boycott.

Representatives of universities and colleges in Tiananmen Square
7:20 P.M., May 21, 1989

Notice to the People of Beijing from Martial Law Headquarters

At ten o'clock, May 20, 1989, by the order of the State Council of the Beijing municipal government, the People's Liberation Army sent troops into certain areas of Beijing to help the local police and the armed police forces.

In order to carry out our tasks successfully, we hereby post the following notice:

1) *The Chinese Liberation Army, under the leadership of the Chinese Communist Party, is a people's army consisting of the sons and brothers of the people. Our only purpose is to serve the people heart and soul. Our divine duty, according to the Constitution, is to defend the motherland and to protect the people so that they may work in a peaceful environment. Our task in Beijing is to maintain order in the capital, not to tackle the students.*

2) *As the troops enforcing martial law carry out their duties, they have encountered some difficulties, but they have exercised enormous restraint and have received the cooperation of the local people. At the moment, Beijing is still in chaos because of traffic jams and a food shortage. A lot of people are concerned with the possibility that security in the capital may deteriorate. The martial law army must carry out its duties firmly and take all measures necessary to reverse the situation. The few criminals who have smashed, attacked, looted, and set fire to public properties will be punished in accordance with the law and the wishes of the people, including those of the patriotic students.*

3) *The People's Liberation Army firmly supports the people's requests to punish guandao, eliminate corruption, and promote socialist democratic progress and the legal system. The purpose of martial law in Beijing is to restore a necessary peaceful environment for the realization of these requests. We believe that the Party and government are capable of responding to the will of the people and taking resolute steps to resolve the problems legally and democratically.*

4) *The martial law army will strictly observe military discipline. In addition, it will begin an education program to promote "love of the capital, of the people, and of the young students" among the soldiers. We will continue the glorious PLA tradition of "supporting the government and loving the people." We oppose any words or deeds that will jeopardize the fish-and-water relationship between the army and people. We will do everything we can to defend the principal interests of the country and people.*

We believe that the people and students in Beijing will display a high level of patriotism and social obligation. They will consider the situation as a whole and support the martial law army with restraint and rationality in order to reach our common goal of restoring order to the capital.

Declaration in Defense of the Constitution

Editor's note: Fifteen well-known Chinese scholars headed by Yan Jiaqi issued a declaration. The following is a condensation of the text.

Because Premier Li Peng imposed martial law in certain areas of Beijing and large numbers of troops have entered the city to stop the students' peaceful democratic movement, strong opposition is growing throughout the nation and has developed into a serious political crisis.

Responding to this emergency situation, we take a common stand and make this request of the CCP and government leaders, of all the people, and of the world.

According to the thirty-fifth item of the Constitution, a Chinese citizen enjoys "freedom of speech, publication, assembly, association, rally, and demonstration." Therefore, it is lawful for the students in Beijing to hold peaceful demonstrations in the Square and to organize inter-college federations. It is also lawful for other citizens to hold personal parties or public gatherings to discuss politics. They should be protected by the Constitution and the law.

Also in accordance with the sixty-seventh item of the Constitution, the Standing Committee of the People's Congress has the authority to supervise the work of the State Council and the Military Commission of the CCP. It was reported in the newspaper that Fei Xiaotong, the vice chairman, and several other members of the Standing Committee of the People's Congress had requested an emergency meeting to discuss the student demonstration. It is time that an emergency meeting of the Standing Committee be held so that it can exercise the authority granted it by the Constitution.

In order to resolve the present crisis, to promote the democratization of Chinese politics, and to continue the policy of open reform and development more effectively, the government must adopt peaceful, legal, and rational approaches to political issues. We demand that the government cancel martial law, which goes against the will of the people, and withdraw the army from Beijing immediately, and that it lose no time in calling the Standing Committee to meeting. It must announce the meeting's agenda at once. Every member present at the meeting should enjoy full rights of initiating a bill and of voting for or against a bill. Ample time should be guaranteed for the meeting's agenda; procedures must be open to the public, and there should be no restrictions on news coverage.

We believe the above measures to be the only ways to resolve the crisis at the moment. Any unlawful, compelling measures would probably lead China into endless confusion and conflict. We recognize the citizens' obligation to protect the Constitution as sacred.

Letter from Ye Fei and Six Other Senior PLA Generals to the Military Commission of the Party and the Martial Law Headquarters

Beijing Martial Law Headquarters:

Please forward this letter to the Military Commission of the CCP. Because of the graveness of the situation in Beijing, we request the following in the name of the old veterans:

The People's Liberation Army is the people's army. It should never stand against its own people. It should never kill its own people, nor should it open fire on its own people. You must not create any bloodshed. To avoid furthering the complicated situation, the army must stay away from the city.

May 21, 1989

May 22, Monday
Massive Forces Surround the City; Government Denies Crackdown

The Central Committee and the State Council demand that the head of the government of each province, each municipality directly under the central government, and each autonomous region take a clear-cut stand in support of Li Peng's speech to the meeting of Party, government, and army cadres on May 19. It is reported that early in the morning, Party and government heads of several areas, including Shanghai, Guangdong, Tianjin, Hubei, Beijing, Jiangxi, and Jiangsu, have already made known their positions in support of Li Peng.

Beijing has been surrounded by a hundred thousand troops from the greater military areas of Shenyang, Jinan, Chengdu, and Beijing. It is reported that a large number of troops have already entered the central areas of the city around Tiananmen Square through underground passages, despite being stopped by citizens on the streets.

Clashes between the army and civilians are heard during the night at Fengtai, a suburb of Beijing, and at Liuli bridge. It is reported that at 10:30 P.M. in Fengtai the soldiers beat up students with belts and bricks and at least forty have been injured.

Deng Yingchao, the widow of the late Zhou Enlai, writes to Beijing students and citizens expressing her concern about the situation in Beijing and calling on the students to return to school at once.

It is rumored that three senior army chiefs, Nie Rongzhen, Xu Xiangqian, and Zhang Aiping, have called on Deng Xiaoping to state that the government should not use the army to deal with the students. It is also rumored that more than a hundred influential senior Party members have written to the Central Committee to oppose the movement of the army into the city and the repression of the students.

Another rumor is widely circulated that five senior commanders have made a united declaration against sending troops into Beijing and are attempting to repress the student movement. The five veteran army leaders are Zhang Aiping, Ye Fei, Sun Shilun, Guo Huaro, and Shu Tong.

The NPC Standing Committee gives its affirmation to the student movement held by all Committee vice-chairmen in Beijing. All present except Wang Hanbin agree that the student movement is positive and that martial law should not be enforced in the city. They also have sent a telegram to Wan Li asking him to return to convene an emergency meeting of the NPC Standing Committee.

Wuer Kaixi spoke through loudspeakers in Tiananmen Square at three in the morning, calling on the students to retreat immediately to the foreign embassy area, saying that this democratic movement is lost. A moment after the speech, he faints. But the decision is attacked by many students, and the Standing Committee therefore decides to remove Wuer from his position as chairman of the FBSU. It is said that he has been taken in by the authorities and believes that the army is coming and that there will be bloodshed.

It is widely rumored that the army will enter the city in the afternoon, and the students decide to persevere to the end. At six

After stopping the troops, people congratulate each other.

P.M. in Tiananmen Square, two hundred thousand students and the teachers who joined them take an oath led by student leader Wang Dan: "Heads may roll, blood may flow, but freedom and democracy must be carried on; we sacrifice our blood and lives, in hope of a better tomorrow for the People's Republic."

The authorities deny that they intend to suppress the students by force and that the government has instructed the sanitation workers to clean the Square tomorrow and has ordered that the main jails be vacated. Meanwhile, the CCTV says that senior army leaders Nie Rongzheng and Xu Xiangqian have refuted rumors about their actions.

Four delegates of the FBSU hand over to the general office of the NPC Standing Committee a "Letter to the Nation," calling on the Standing Committee of the NPC to hold an emergency meeting. A "Letter to Comrade Deng Xiaoping" is also drafted by the FBSU, the students' headquarters in Tiananmen Square, the headquarters of students from other parts of China, and the hunger strike group.

The Beijing Workers' Autonomous Union is considering a general strike in Beijing to force the government to make concessions.

Ten well-known intellectuals issue "The Oath of Intellectuals," determining not to yield to the high-handed policy of the government and to take a firm stand in support of the students. The ten intellectuals are Bao Zunxin, Yan Jiaqi, Su Xiaokang, Wang Juntao, Sheng Dade, Wu Tingjia, Ming Qi, Chen Xiaoping, Li Dewei, and Xie Xiaoqing.

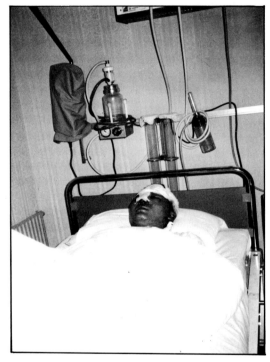

Soldier wounded in the Fengtai incident.

Reporters visit the striking students.

Citizens organize a dare-to-die corps.

107

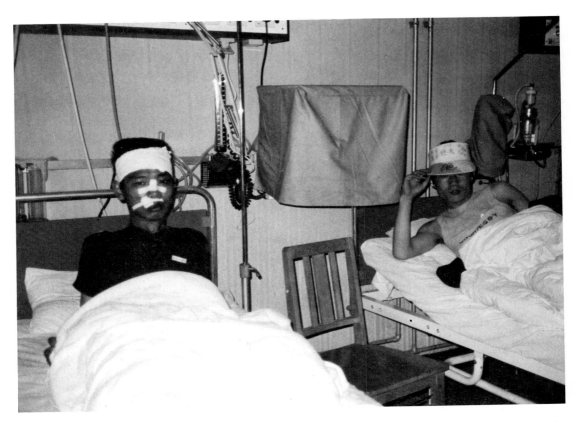

Students wounded in the Fengtai incident.

We shall not fall and make the butchers tall. Let the wind of freedom blow and blow (by Beidao).

Wang Roshui, a well-known intellectual, marches in the street after his return from the U.S.

Some ten thousand professionals demonstrate in the streets in spite of the martial law, carrying banners reading "Step down, Li Peng" and "Oppose martial law and the army take over," and calling for a city-wide demonstration. Those present include Wang Roshui, a literary critic; Lao Gui, the author of *Bloody Sunset*; Dai Qing, a journalist, and Zhao Yu.

Wan Li will not change the schedule for his eleven-day official visit to the United States, it is said.

People outside Beijing continue to show their support for the Beijing students. Demonstrations are still taking place in Nanjing, Shanghai, Xian, Guangzhou, and Shenzhen. In England and in Macao, rallies are held in support of the Beijing students.

The Federation of Beijing Intellectuals is established on May 20.

Well-known writers Zhao Yu (in white shirt) and Zheng Yi (left).

Beijing College and University Students' Open Letter to the People of the Whole Nation

Our dear compatriots,

The situation in Tiananmen Square is deteriorating. In view of all possible outcomes, we believe that it is imperative that we, the college and university students of Beijing, make the following announcement.

First, the current situation was caused entirely by the erroneous decisions of the top leaders. The inhuman indifference and cruelty these leaders have demonstrated in their treatment of our hunger strike and petition have aroused tremendous indignation among people all over the country. The decision-makers at the State Council should bear full responsibility for whatever grave consequences arise.

Second, in the light of the undesirable behavior of Yang Shangkun, chairman of the PRC, and Li Peng, premier of the State Council, during the course of the students' hunger strike and petition, we believe that they have lost the basic qualities that a Communist and a state leader must possess. Therefore, we propose that the NPC Standing Committee immediately remove Yang Shangkun and Li Peng from all the government posts that they now hold; we also propose that the CCP Central Committee depose Yang Shangkun and Li Peng and expel them from the Party. Article No. 187 of the Criminal Law of the PRC indicates that "All persons in the civil service who bring damage to public property or harm to the interests of the country or the people because of dereliction of duty should be punished." Now that Yang Shangkun and Li Peng have proven with deeds their dereliction of duty, we present our accusation to the Supreme People's Procuratorate of China and request its public prosecution of these men.

As chairman of CCP Military Commission, Deng Xiaoping places himself above the state and the Party, in total violation of the third item under Article No. 10 of the Constitution of the CCP, which says, "The highest governing body of the CCP is the National Congress of the Party and its control Committee." He practices feudal dictatorship, totally violating Article No. 16 of the Constitution of the CCP, which says, "No individual should be allowed to exercise absolute power and place himself above the organization." His counter-revolutionary scheme of using military forces to suppress the masses totally violates Article No. 131 of the Criminal Law of the PRC, which states, "A citizen's personal rights, right to democracy, and other rights are under legal protection from violation by any other persons or any institutions," and directly violates the CCP Constitution. We propose that the CCP Central Committee depose Deng Xiaoping from all Party posts that he holds and expel him from the Party. We hereby present our accusation to the Supreme People's Procuratorate of China and request that it publicly prosecute him.

Third, the on-going student movement is a great patriotic movement. The sole aim of its more than one hundred thousand participants is the demand for democratic administration. We ask for nothing but a prosperous and strong China. We oppose any words and deeds that harm our country and the people. Therefore, we strongly protest the current government's hideous measures, which have aggravated the situation and brought about nationwide turmoil. For the support and assistance we have received from the broad masses of the people, we hereby express our most heartfelt gratitude and warmest welcome. Since the situation is rapidly becoming worse, we strongly appeal to the people to remain calm and orderly so that our struggle can be reasonable and move effectively in the right direction.

Fourth, we have no intention at all of being involved in a sectarian conflict within the Party, as we think that the immediate problem China is facing is to establish a democratic system with complete law and order. There is no need at all for us to base all our hopes for the future of China on one or two individuals; the traditional concept of one extraordinary premier who can deliver the rank and file from oppression should be done away with completely. So we strongly urge the birth of an autonomous democratic organization based on unity among intellectuals, workers, and all citizens. Such an organization, we trust, completely conforms to the Constitution and to the will of the people, and it is intended to effectively supervise and restrain the government and the ruling parties. Not until such an organization comes into existence can we claim that the students' struggle for democracy has come to a successful end.

Our dear compatriots, this is a cruel moment for our nation. History gives us a very small chance; so let all honest, compassionate, and patriotic people step forward; with our common effort, a democratic and free, strong and thriving China will surely be born!

Open Letter to Comrade Deng Xiaoping

Dear Xiaoping,
    Greetings.
    In response to the call from college and university students, a patriotic mass movement on an unprecedented scale has emerged in Beijing and in many other parts of the country demanding democracy and opposing corruption. Some top leaders, deaf to the people's voice and blind to their own errors, regard this patriotic movement as "turmoil" and have summoned troops into the city of Beijing. Martial law has been in effect for more than twenty-four hours. However, demonstrations still go on continuously in Beijing. Thanks to the persuasion of honest citi-

zens, the troops are still outside the city, finding no chance of entry at all. Never before have orders from the Central Committee encountered such resistance. Wise as you are, you are not unaware of the current situation, nor of the way people feel about it. Though some demonstrators did shout slogans that humiliated you, we believe they spoke from anger and resentment; people will never forget the remarkable contributions you have made to the country, which we regret not being able to discuss in detail. What people resent is that you, who are seen both in China and throughout the world as China's leading statesman, should fail to judge the current democratic movement sensibly. We admit that there has been some turmoil in Beijing, and we anxiously hope that this turmoil will be ended as soon as possible. It should be noted, however, that the masses are determined to seek democracy and oppose corruption and that they will never compromise with the current government, which misinterprets the nature of this patriotic movement. Thus, we assume that the confrontation between the government and the people is to continue and that the turmoil will not come to an end and that restoration of stability seems remote.

In view of such a situation, we sense that in order to accomplish the goal of this movement peacefully, in a country where genuine democracy has not yet been fully realized, the mission, or perhaps the historical opportunity, has befallen you once again. We beseech you to use your

reputation and charisma in the Party, government, and armed forces to press for the resignation of certain unpopular leaders in order to reestablish an honest administration that wholeheartedly serves the people. In a sense, this democratic movement is a turning point in the history of China. We believe that you are able to grasp the true nature of this hard-fought national movement for the people. What is to be written on this page of our history will be determined by your decision. It is our sincere and earnest hope that with your involvement a large stride in the course of democracy in China can be made nonviolently. This would surely be one of the most remarkable contributions of your long and distinguished career. Your support is needed to make China a prosperous and strong country with genuine democracy and freedom.

Disaster is right around the corner; so please, Comrade Deng Xiaoping, make a speedy decision.

Signed by Commanding Headquarters in Tiananmen Square

Recovered Leaders of the Hunger Strike

Beijing Federation of Colleges and Universities

Commanding Headquarters of Universities from Other Cities

A Pledge by Some Intellectuals
May 22, 1989

Being intellectuals, we hereby solemnly pledge on our consciences, on our bodies and souls, and on our dignity as humans that we will never betray the pro-democratic cause that the patriotic students have defended with their

blood and lives. We will not look for excuses for our cowardice. We will not tolerate past humiliations. We will not sell out conscience, nor submit to dictatorship. We will never be subordinate to the last emperor of China.

Defaced portrait of Mao on the rostrum of Tiananmen.

May 23, Tuesday

Mao's portrait on the Tiananmen Gate is defaced when three men throw eggs and red, yellow, white, and black paint at it. Alert students catch the three, question them, and take them to the police. The three men claim to be a journalist, a teacher, and a worker from Hunan. But this is dubious since they speak in fluent Beijing dialect, and none of them speaks Hunan dialect. Immediately after the vandalism, someone covers the portrait with a huge military canvas. The students are suspicious because they think the huge canvas, five meters by three meters, would have been hard to find so quickly if it were not ready beforehand.

Citizens give the soldiers food.

Citizens working with students to keep order in Tiananmen Square.

During the night, the stained portrait is replaced by a new one.

It is rumored that the Li Peng circle, including the Beijing Municipal Committee of the CCP and the propaganda guiding group under Li Peng, is sorting out the "black materials" of Zhao Ziyang, in preparation to build a case against him.

About fifty members of the NPC Standing Committee have signed a proposal to convene a special meeting, but the proposal needs thirty more signatures to be formally raised.

Deng Yingchao, the widow of the late Zhou Enlai, denies the rumor that she will withdraw from the Party if the authorities suppress the students. In her "Letter to Beijing Students and Citizens" she calls on the students and other people to trust the party, the government, and the People's

Liberation Army. She also says that the army is coming to restore order in Beijing.

The Beijing Municipal Committee of the Party and the PLA Headquarters for the Enforcement of Martial Law release an announcement demanding the restoration of order in Beijing as soon as possible.

Fifteen student picketers from Beijing Normal are beaten up by soldiers with no insignias on their caps when the students try to dissuade the troops from entering the city at Fushouling subway station. Some of the students are missing.

Army spies sneak into the sit-in, and one of them is picked out by protestors. The spy is later released.

According to the Beijing Public Security Bureau, the crime rate in the city during April and May falls to the lowest of the year.

Wan Li talks about the student movements in China during his visit to Canada. He states that the government should protect the students' patriotism and, at the same time, maintain social stability.

May 24, Wednesday
Six Greater Military Areas Make Known Their Support of Li Peng

The new student leaders, the Tiananmen Square Security Headquarters, take an oath of office. Chai Ling is still the chair of the headquarters, and she is responsible directly to the joint conference of the hunger strike group, the FBSU dialogue delegation, student representatives of the main colleges and universities in and outside Beijing, and several non-student elements. Wang Dan, the moderator of the joint conference, reads the statement of the conference, pointing out that no matter how this student movement ends, it will certainly be one of the most glorious events in Chinese history.

Wang Dan claims that the Beijing Municipal Government and the Municipal Committee of the CCP should be responsive to the disorder in Beijing. He says that the Beijing government has juggled things to paralyze the city and create a food shortage.

High-ranking Party and government officials are to meet in Beijing. Except for Wan Li, who is still on his visit to the United States, the members of the CCP Political Bureau and the governmental heads of every province, city, and autonomous district have arrived in Beijing. Members of the Political Bureau meet and discuss the issues raised by the student movement. A top-level power struggle is said to be under discussion, and one of the solutions suggested

at the meeting is that Li Peng and Zhao Ziyang both step down.

Veteran general Ye Fei strikes the table and verbally attacks Li Peng at the joint meeting of the NPC Standing Committee. He claims that the achievements of forty years of hard work have been ruined overnight by Li Peng.

The Li Peng circle is active. A special commission formed by Yuan Mu, He Dongchang, Zeng Jianhui, Wang Renzhi, and Li Zhimin briefs media heads in a meeting that lasts four hours.

Wan Li, chairman of the NPC Standing Committee, cuts short his stay in the United States and returns to China, but the Xinhua news says that Wan Li's early return is due to health concerns. Peng Chong, assistant secretary general of the NPC, says that a call for an NPC emergency meeting is subject to ratification by the Central Committee of the CCP. "What can we do if there are different opinions at the meeting or if the resolution of the meeting is not in line with the Central Committee?" Peng Chong adds.

A large number of troops arrive in Beijing by armored carriers, trains, and airplanes, and those troops move from the city station to the suburbs of Beijing. A high-ranking army officer says that the reason for their coming is the power struggle in the

Student leaders Wang Dan (center) and Chai Ling (inset).

Party, not the student movement.

Six greater military areas out of seven (the other is Beijing) make their support for Li Peng known. The general offices of the PLA, the navy, and the air force also express their support. The *PLA News* publishes a letter from the headquarters of the General Staff and the General Political Department urging the martial law troops to learn of Yang Shangkun's and Li Peng's speeches. The army leaders also urge the soldiers to read the April 26 editorial of the *People's Daily*.

Another rumor claims that the news that Li Peng and Zhao Ziyang have been removed from their positions is not true and that the Central Committee has not met yet.

In Beijing, satellite transmission had been resumed the previous day, but the post office once again cut off fax and satellite at five P.M. this evening.

The Guangdong, Hong Kong, and Macao

Six hundred thousand people from Guangdong, Hong Kong, and Macao march in Guangzhou on May 24.

massive demonstration takes place in Guangzhou. Six hundred thousand people march on Guangzhou's main streets. A rumor circulates during the demonstration that Li Peng has stepped down.

According to a news agency in Hong Kong, thirty-six well-known Chinese-American scientists and academics, including Cheng-ning Yang, Yuen-che Li, Sheng-shen Ch'en, and Chien-hsiung Wu, have sent a telegram to Deng Xiaoping on May 21, appealing to him to withdraw the troops, avoid bloodshed, and convene an emergency NPC Standing Committee meeting to discuss Li Peng.

Without the people's support, the tank becomes a "paper tiger."

May 25, Thursday

The Tiananmen Square Security Headquarters meets with representative students from more than three hundred colleges and universities to discuss the next action it will take. The four plans being considered are: 1) further actions to push the government even harder by, for instance, enlarging the hunger strike and/or calling on workers to stage a general strike; 2) negotiation with the government while continuing the hunger strike with the possibility of retreating from the Square under certain conditions; 3) continuation of the hunger strike in the Square but no negotiation with the government, holding on and waiting for an answer from the government; 4) letting the hunger strike run its course, with the headquarters ceasing to give directions with each college and university deciding whether or not its students will stay.

Wan Li concludes his visit in the United States several days early and returns to China, but he stops at Shanghai and does not go to Beijing.

Li Peng shows up for the first time since his May 19 speech. At a meeting in Zhongnanhai, the headquarters of the CCP Central Committee, Li Peng tells ambassadors of Nigeria, Mexico, and Burma that disturbances are taking place in some parts of China, but the government is stable and capable of solving the problem. The People's Liberation Army, Li adds, exercised great restraint and avoided clashes while entering the nation's capital city. He stresses that "the standard-bearer of China's reform is Deng Xiaoping, not anyone else."

Initiated by the professional circle and the Beijing Workers' Autonomous Union, a million people demonstrate in Beijing once again. Students and other people also participate in the demonstration. Some officers of the State System Reform Commission under Li Peng take part in the march, too.

Beijing citizens organize a dare-to-die corps to protect the striking students.

Demonstrations in support of the Beijing students take place in eight large cities in China, including Shanghai, Tianjin, Nanjing, Wuhan, Changsha, Chengdu, Xian, and Guangzhou. In Shanghai and Tianjin tens of thousands of people take to the streets.

Everybody is eager for information, and the bulletin board is always crowded.

The bus is painted with a slogan against Li Peng.

Zhao seems to have lost power less than ten days after his meeting with Gorbachev.

May 26, Friday
Zhao Ziyang Dismissed on Charges of Five Offenses

The leadership of the striking students decides to take new action against the authorities. After discussion of the four possible plans mentioned above, the representative students from thirty colleges and universities vote in Tiananmen Square to decide the next step of the student movement. They choose the first of the four schemes, and it is decided that the students will continue their occupation of Tiananmen Square and at the same time organize a larger demonstration or hunger strike and call for the workers' general strike.

Top leaders of the Central Committee informally make Zhao's dismissal known to high-ranking officials. In high-level Party and government organs, informal talks are held to criticize Zhao's wrongdoings since the death of Hu Yaobang. Zhao's five major offenses are: 1) Immediately following Hu's death, some people demanded that the Party leadership and the government announce Hu's rehabilitation and reject the opposing bourgeois liberalization campaign. The Central Committee should have actively spoken out and guided public opinion in the right direction. The Central Committee failed to do so because Zhao Ziyang had a different opinion and emphasized restraint on the part of the Party. 2) Before Zhao left to visit North Korea, he

delegated his responsibility to Li Peng and the State Council, demanding that order be restored, close attention be paid to dialogue, and bloodshed be avoided. Later, when the situation was becoming severe, Li Peng called a meeting of the Politburo's Standing Committee, reported to Deng Xiaoping, and decided that the nature of the events was disorderly. But the organs under Zhao made the "Announcement of Six Points," trying to place the Central Committee and the State Council on trial before the National People's Congress. 3) Zhao acted arbitrarily and put himself above the Party Central Committee, thereby committing the same error as the late Hu Yaobang. In particular, he leaked a Party secret when he met with Soviet leader Gorbachev; he, by his own decision, saw the striking students in Tiananmen Square and made statements not suited to his position as general secretary of the Central Committee. 4) Zhao is the man behind this disturbance, and the State System Reform Commission is his special detachment. Zhao incited students to create turmoil so that he could grasp power in the Party and the government. 5) Both Deng Xiaoping and Li Peng were self-critical and took responsibility for errors in the economy, but Zhao did not.

Yan Mingfu and Li Tieying are named as new members of the Standing Committee of the Political Bureau of the CCP Central Committee. Yan Mingfu, minister of the United Front Department of the CCP, is Zhao's man and has some influence among the intellectuals. It is believed that this arrangement is meant to console Zhao and his men.

Peng Zhen, former chairman of the NPC Standing Committee, invites some members of that committee who belong to the Chinese democratic parties (which are under the leadership of the CCP and subject to its instructions) to a forum. Peng's speech at the meeting emphasizes that the "unusual methods" adopted by the government are entirely in accord with the Constitution and the law. He also repeats that the events in Beijing are disturbances and reaffirms the "people's democratic dictatorship" and socialist system.

The Standing Committee of the Central Advisory Commission of the CCP expresses its firm support of Li Peng's and Yang Shangkun's May 19 speeches. Chen Yun, a senior Party leader and chairman of the Commission, presides over the meeting. Among those present are Bo Yibo and Song Renqiong, both vice-chairmen of the committee, and standing members Wang Ping, Wang Shoudao, Wu Xiuquan, Liu Lantao, Jiang Hua, Yang Dezhi, Xiao Ke, Yu Qiuli, Song Shilun, Zhang Jinfu, Lu Dingyi, Chen Peixian, Chen Xilian, Hu Qiaomu, Duan Junyi, Geng Biao, Ji Pengfei, Huang Zhen, Kang Shien, and Huang Huoqing.

The Beijing greater military area finally expresses its support of Li Peng and his decision to put Beijing under martial law. Thus, all of the seven greater military areas have shown their support of Li Peng.

It is rumored that there will be purges in three "black nests" and in the main organs of the government, including the PLA's General Staff headquarters, General Political Department, and General Logistics Department, the ministries and commissions under the State Council, the main organs and productive units directly under the central government, and the Party organizations that did not take a clear-cut stand in favor of the April 26 editorial of the *People's Daily*. The three "black nests" are the PLA's General Staff headquarters, Beijing University, and the Chinese Academy of Social Sciences. It is reported that people who have actively taken part in the disturbance will be purged.

May 27, Saturday

At a joint conference of the FBSU, the organizations of students from other parts of China, and the organizations of other circles, it is decided that the striking students will withdraw from Tiananmen Square on May 30 and there will be an all-Beijing demonstration and a mass rally in Tiananmen Square. Wang Dan, head of the Beida Autonomous Student Union, declares a ten point announcement on behalf of the Federation of Beijing Autonomous Student Unions, the joint conference of other sections of work in Beijing, the headquarters of students from other parts of the country, the Workers' Autonomous Union, and the Citizens' Autonomous Union.

Tsen Chienshiun, director of the concert.

119

Wan Li, chairman of the NPC Standing Committee, expresses his support of Li Peng's May 19 speech and announces that the National People's Congress will be held around June 20. Li Xiannian, chairman of the Chinese People's Political Consultative Conference (CPPCC), also expresses his firm support of Li Peng's and Yang Shangkun's May 19 speeches and their decision to enforce martial law in Beijing.

A Hong Kong arts circle holds a "concert for democracy in China" that lasts for twelve hours. The concert attracts approximately three hundred thousand citizens and raises more than twelve million Hong Kong dollars. The donations will go to the foundation of the Hong Kong Democratic Movement League and will be used for activities in Hong Kong or mainland China to support the Beijing student movement.

The Association of Chinese Students in France calls for a "great march of Chinese all over the world" at ten A.M. on May 28. It is hoped that the great march will take place in China as well as in other countries.

Wang Mingchuan, a TV star and a deputy to the People's Congress, singing.

In Hong Kong, the "Concert for Democracy in China" is attended by three hundred thousand people and raises twelve million H.K. dollars.

Lu KuanTin, composer with his wife of the song "For Freedom."

Hou Derchien, a composer, singing.

Deng Lejiun, a famous singer, sings with tears in her eyes.

Ch'eng Lung and other stars perform.

The theme of the concert is "For Freedom."

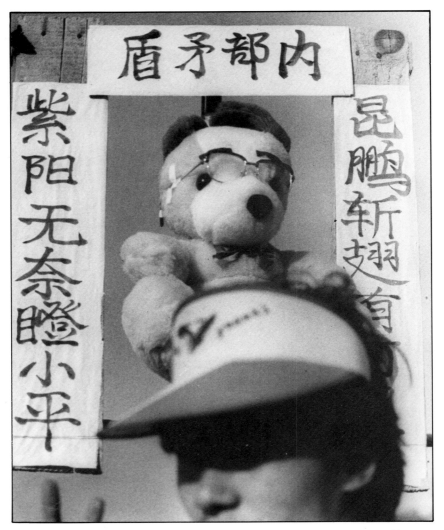

A cartoon suggests that the people don't want the democratic movement to be exploited by party politicians and that the Party leaders are all the same.

A Joint Ten-Point Statement
May 27, 1989

The ten thousand student participants of the sit-down demonstration in Tiananmen Square held a joint meeting with representatives of other organizations of the city and of the student federation of universities and colleges in Beijing on the eighth day after the government declared martial law. Yesterday a press conference was given for both Chinese and foreign news reporters at which the students announced the conclusion of the sit-down strike on Tuesday,

May 30, the eleventh day after the declaration of martial law. They also announced plans for another city-wide peaceful demonstration and a rally in the Square.

Present at the conference were student leaders Wang Dan, chairman of the Beida Autonomous Student Union; Chai Ling, chief commander in the Square headquarters of Beijing Normal Branch; and Wuer Kaixi, a university student representative.

Wang Dan, on behalf of all the organizations that attended the joint meeting, read a ten-point statement. The following is a condensed version.

1) The spontaneous student movement has developed into a widespread, patriotic campaign for democracy. Because the movement has already ignited political struggles within the Party, the democratic forces it represents will not be stopped.

2) Whoever takes power in the government must be in accord with the people, set democracy as his starting point, and reform the political system to make it democratic.

3) Future leaders of China will be judged by their attitudes toward democratic patriotism. Pro-democratic leaders will be supported by the people; those who are against democracy will be abandoned.

4) It is not wise for Li Peng, He Dongchang, Yuan Mu, and Li Ximin to adopt a negative attitude toward the patriotic and democratic student movement. They have demonstrated their inability to serve as China's major leaders. Having Li Peng in office is a great danger to the safety of workers, civilians, officials, and those Party members who have shown their support of the student movement.

5) Zhao Ziyang, the general secretary of the Party, is supportive of the movement; he should remain in his office.

6) No official who loses his office because of his negative attitude toward the movement should hold a grudge toward the students.

7) This movement is, as stated, a spontaneous campaign, patriotic and democratic in nature, by the students and the people. It is by no means a political struggle inside the Party.

8) Whatever the outcome of the Party struggle, martial law must be lifted, the army must be withdrawn from the city of Beijing, the April 26 editorial by the People's Daily must be refuted as must Li Peng's speech on May 20, 1989, and an emergency meeting of the Standing Committee of the People's Congress must be held immediately to discuss the proposal to remove Li Peng from office.

9) On May 30, the eleventh day after martial law was ordered, we shall withdraw from Tiananmen Square after a mass rally.

10) April 27 should be observed as a Day of Democracy and Liberty for China.

May 28, Sunday

Students in Beijing respond to the "great march of Chinese all over the world." However, the march in Beijing is not as big as hoped, for officials at all levels, including those in the mass media, have put pressure on their subordinates and warned them not to join the march.

Overseas Chinese take part in the great march in Taibei (Taiwan), Gaoxiong (Taiwan), Macao, Osaka, San Francisco, Los Angeles, and Sydney.

In Hong Kong, one and a half million people take to the streets in a march around the city that is even larger than the May 21 demonstration. Many of the participants are from unions and media close to the Communist Party. Led by Situ Hua and Martin Li, the demonstration sets off from the central district and lasts for eight hours.

Martin Lee, a deputy of the Hong Kong legislature, who organized and led the march.

One and a half million people march in Hong Kong to support demonstrations in China.

A child holding a flag, which reads "democracy."

A caricature of Li Peng.

May 29, Monday

The Beijing student leaders collectively resign because they feel they cannot settle the dispute between the organizations of Beijing students and those of students from outside Beijing. Chai Ling, general director of the Safeguard Tiananmen Square Headquarters, and four other members of the headquarters' standing committee are among those who resign.

The students decide to postpone their withdrawal from the Square until June 20,

the day the National People's Congress is scheduled to convene.

Units and departments of the Party and the government assert their loyalty to the Central Committee.

In Shanghai, the autonomous student union calls for a school boycott action, requesting students leave school and not return until September 1, the beginning of the next semester.

Wang Dan resigns.

Chai Ling resigns.

Student strikers from other parts of the country insist that the sit-down protest continue until June 20.

Students build the framework for the Goddess of Democracy.

The Goddess of Democracy, ten meters tall, on Tiananmen Square.

The Goddess of Democracy confronts Mao's figure. How long can they co-exist?

About one thousand students and workers come to the Beijing Public Security Bureau demanding the release of the three workers arrested by the police.

May 30, Tuesday

The "goddess of democracy" is put up in Tiananmen Square. The figure of the goddess, ten meters tall, attracts tens of thousands of people.

Sheng Yingeng, Qian Yumin, and Bai Dongping, members of the Beijing Workers' Autonomous Union, are taken away by public security police. The Xinhua news reports that the eleven members of the electric bicycle team, which has helped to transfer

information for the striking students, are detained by police. Nearly a thousand students and workers demonstrate in front of the Beijing Public Security Bureau demanding the release of the workers.

A joint conference of Beijing workers announces a statement praising the student movement as a purely patriotic pro-democracy movement that has nothing to do with any political groups. The students decide to

127

leave the date open for their withdrawal from the Square. The students also decide that they will resume dialogues with the government and retreat from the Square only after the government responds to their four conditions, which are: 1) to rescind the martial law; 2) to remove the army from Beijing; 3) to guarantee not to "settle accounts after the autumn harvest"; and 4) to fulfill freedom of the press as guaranteed in the Constitution.

May 31, Wednesday

The *People's Daily* publishes a statement from the Tiananmen Square Management Office indicating that the students put the figure of the "goddess of democracy" in the Square illegally. Students from the Central Academy of Fine Arts say that the Management Office did not contact them. At ten o'clock in the morning, a man climbs up the framework of the figure and tries to push it over. The man is taken away by the students and sent to the students' headquarters, but is later released.

The students' headquarters in Tiananmen Square decides to reorganize the order in the Square. Guo Haifeng, a member of its Standing Committee, is appointed director of the reorganization. It is decided that all the old, crude tents will be replaced by new tents that are gifts from Hong Kong. After the change, 3,500 students can stay in the new tents.

A group of more than ten military motorcycles followed by a military jeep patrols Beijing's main streets in the early morning.

The police organize a pro-government march in the suburbs of Beijing. Several thousand citizens participate in the march.

Some foreign news media guess that this is a warning that the government is about to lose its patience.

Thousands of peasants, cadres, students, and other people march in the suburbs of Beijing in support of the government. The march is approved by the authorities and takes place in Ro, Fengtai, and Daxin counties in the southern suburbs of Beijing. The demonstrators shout "down with Fang Lizhi" and other slogans in support of the government. After the march, the crowd burns two figures representing well-known Chinese physician and dissenter Fang Lizhi and a "conspirator." Zhou Xing, the organizer of the march, says, "some troublemakers want to put pressure on the government. Fang Lizhi is one of them." Witnesses report that the demonstrators receive ice cream and drinks from the government after the march.

Three thousand students march in Tiananmen Square in the evening to protest the Public Security Bureau's arrest of the three leaders of the Workers' Autonomous Union. Later, the students and several thousand workers demonstrate in front of the Beijing Public Security Bureau, demanding the reason for the arrest. The demonstrators shout slogans such as "workers and students, fight for democracy together," and "oppose kidnapping." The police warn them to obey the martial law and to leave at once. According to the leader of the Beijing Workers' Autonomous Union, the three arrested workers had already been released at five that evening.

At night, more than a thousand people demonstrate in front of the Xinhuamen Gate, shouting, "Down with Li Peng," and, "Long live democracy." The police do not take actions against the demonstrators, but officials push away foreign reporters and television cameras.

June 1, Thursday

At three A.M. Chai Ling, general director of the Tiananmen Square Headquarters, and her husband Feng Congde are the subjects of a kidnapping attempt. Because of Feng Congde's resistance, the kidnapping fails and the perpetrators run away. The kidnappers are Lian Shengde, member of the Federation of Autonomous Student Unions from outside Beijing, Huang Wen and Chen Wei, both students from other parts of the country, and another man who looks like a worker, Chai Ling tells reporters later in the morning. Chai Ling states she will not shrink back, but she also expresses her suspicion that some of the students have been bribed by the authorities. Meanwhile, Li Lu, deputy director of the student headquarters in the Square, says that in the early morning while Zhang Jian, head of the students' pickets, was drunk, two loudspeakers on the Monument and the only telephone in the headquarters had been cut off.

The *People's Daily* publishes an article speaking highly of the late leader Hu Yaobang. The article, entitled "Hu Yaobang's Contributions to the Rectification," says that during Hu's term as head of the Organization Department of the CCP Central Committee after the Cultural Revolution, he reversed many wrong decisions of the Gang of Four and rescued many people persecuted and sentenced for unnamed crimes during that period. He also made retributions to thousands of wronged officials and rehabilitated a hundred thousand rightists, the article says. Especially, the report continues, he broke through many barriers and produced the "Report on the Case of the 'Sixty-One People' "; as a result, the case of the so-called sixty-one traitors was set right after twelve years of injustice, and the people falsely convicted, including Bo Yibo, Liu Lantao, and An Ziwen, were rescued from unjust treatment.

Deng Xiaoping and Hu Yaobang at the Sixth Plenary Session of the Twelfth Central Committee.

Children play on the square on Children's Day.

Chai Ling and her husband Feng Congde.

Sanitation vehicle sprays the Square.

Students help clean up garbage on the Square.

The huge banner says, "Take a firm stand against bourgeois 'democracy.' "

Many large hotels in Beijing hang out huge streamers in support of the authorities during the night. One streamer, hanging down from the seventh floor of Jianguo Hotel, reads, "Take a firm stand against bourgeois 'democracy'." Another reads, "Support the great, glorious, and correct Chinese Communist Party."

June 1 is Children's Day in China, and the atmosphere in the Square is calm. Many parents take their children to the Square to see what is happening. It is quiet in the Square. Garbage workers are cleaning up the place while the students work replacing the tents.

The Federation of Beijing Autonomous Student Unions (FBSU), the Federation of Autonomous Student Unions from outside of Beijing (FASU), and the student headquarters in Tiananmen Square hold a news conference in front of the Monument to the People's Heroes, stating that the patriotic and democratic movement is not to be influenced by the power struggle in the Party, and the goals of the movement remain the same, that is, to achieve democracy and freedom through peaceful dialogue. They repeat their four demands and say that if the government accepts these conditions they will carry out an open and equal dialogue with the government. The four preconditions include calling off martial law, withdrawing troops from Beijing, insuring no punishment is inflicted in any form on the participants of the democratic movement, and discontinuing news censorship. The students say that if these basic demands cannot be satisfied they are determined to persist in the protest to the end, despite the risk of being killed. Observers notice that those four demands do not include the condemnation of the April 26 editorial of the *People's Daily*.

At a press conference, Foreign Ministry spokesman Li Jinhua denies the rumor that Deng Xiaoping is sick and hospitalized and says that the rumor is a fabrication of someone with ulterior motives. Li says that no personnel changes have been made in the leadership of the Party, the government, the army, or the National Congress. At the conclusion of the news conference, the Beijing Municipal Government spokesman Din Weijun repeats the "Beijing Municipal Government Order" of May 20 and explains to Chinese and foreign journalists the following seven points:

1) During the period of martial law, journalists from abroad as well as from Hong Kong, Macao, and Taiwan must apply to the foreign affairs office of the municipal government for a permit if they intend to cover the news in Beijing.

2) Both the second item of Beijing Municipal Government Order No. 2 and the second item of the Government Order No. 3 ban the foreign, Hong Kong, Taiwan, and Macao journalists from interviewing, photographing, or videotaping activities prohibited by the Beijing government in Tiananmen Square, around the Great Hall of the People, at Xinhuamen Gate, and in other public places. The journalists are not allowed to take Chinese citizens to their stations, apartments, or hotel rooms for interviews about the activities that are prohibited by the Beijing government.

3) Foreign, Hong Kong, Macao, and Taiwan journalists are not allowed to interview, photograph, or videotape the martial law troops without the permission of the Beijing government.

4) Foreign, Hong Kong, Macao, and Taiwan journalists are prohibited from obtaining, through illegal channels, materials that may incite people and that are banned during the martial law period.

5) During the enforcement of martial law, the Beijing Municipal Government orders may override any other relevant regulations with which they may come into conflict.

6) Violators of the Beijing Municipal Government Orders will be punished according to the degree of seriousness by the appropriate departments of the Beijing government.

7) The Beijing Municipal Government reserves the authority to interpret the municipal government orders.

The FBSU reorganized its leading group last night. Wuer Kaixi and Wang Dan are no longer members of the Standing Committee. The new committee is formed by representatives from nine schools: Beida, Qinghua, the People's University, the University of Aviation and Aeronautics, Political Science and Law, Beijing Normal, Central Nationalities, Beijing Economics, and the Graduate School of the Chinese Academy of Social Science.

Overseas Chinese journalists welcomed by the people.

An American journalist reports from Tiananmen Square on the seventh day of martial law.

June 2, Friday
Army Surrounds the City; Police Car Kills People

It is said that about two hundred thousand troops are stationed around the city, and some of them are trying to enter the center of Beijing. Meanwhile, the army has taken control of the major media, including the television station, radio station, telegraph office, and post office. In the early morning, more than ten thousand troops try to break into Tiananmen Square from Changan Boulevard but are stopped near the Beijing Hotel by hundreds and thousands of students and citizens. Crowds jam the street, and the troops and the civilians push among each other; the chaos lasts until around three A.M.; then the troops retreat.

Around midnight or in the early morning, a police car without license plates speeds through Fuxingmenwai Street. The car runs into a tricycle, crushes it, then dashes onto the sidewalk and hits four peo-ple. At least two of them die immediately, one of them a woman teacher at the Mining Institute. A citizen almost hit by the car accuses the police of speeding, but the police reply, "Get out of our way. We're in a hurry." Civilians lose no time in taking the victims to the hospital. In the next few minutes, another police car comes to the two trouble-makers' aid and takes them away. Witnesses say that before the accident many police jeeps had sped through the streets like that. In the wrecked police car, people find clubs, knives, and uniforms of the armed police. Thousands of citizens, agitated by the policemen's departure after killing the people, spontaneously demonstrate in Tiananmen Square; they later join other people in placing obstacles to block the troops trying to enter the Square.

A large group of soldiers trying to reach Tiananmen Square.

Peasants on the outskirts of Beijing hold demonstrations in support of the Li Peng government. After the pro-authority demonstration two days before in the countryside south of Beijing, the Beijing Municipal Government once again organizes peasants in the streets of Miyun and Changping counties to support the Li Peng government. Demonstrators shout slogans after cadres: "Stick to the four basic principles," "Be firm in support of the wise decision of the Central Committee," and "How are you, Deng Xiaoping?" A participant re-

veals that those who attended the government-organized demonstration received ten Chinese dollars, a straw hat, and two days paid leave.

From Beida, Beijing Normal, and Beijing Agriculture, about a thousand students stage a satire march in the streets. They wear tall paper hats with the words "monsters and demons" on them, like the hats worn by "counter-revolutionaries" in parades of punishment during the Cultural Revolution. The students shout ironic slogans such as, "Support dictatorship, support despotism," and, "Martial law is enforced; demonstrations are in order; everybody gets ten dollars. Say you support Li Peng." The parade passes through Changan Boulevard and attracts many bystanders. When the citizens realize that this is satire, they clap their hands and cheer the students.

Hou Derchien, a famous popular music composer; Liu Xiaobo, Ph.D., a lecturer in the Chinese department of Beijing Normal; Zhou Tuo, head of the General Planning Department of the Si Tong Company; and Gao Xin, a member of the Chinese Communist Party and former chief editor of the *Normal University Weekly*, start a seventy-two hour hunger strike in Tiananmen Square. Hou Derchien, one of the four members, will fast forty-eight hours because he will be leaving for Hong Kong on Sunday. The four announce the "June 2 Hunger Strike Declaration," expressing that this hunger strike is not a petition but a protest against martial law and military patrolling. The declaration, on one hand, denounces the government's mistakes in handling the student movement; on the other hand, it criticizes the non-democratic elements in the students' activities. The document calls for calm and introspection on both sides in order to seek solutions to the crisis. Hou Derchien says that his hunger strike represents more than a hundred Hong Kong singers and stars.

Delegates of the Hong Kong Democratic Movement League say that this student uprising is a patriotic movement, not chaos, and so they will continue to support the students with materials and money. Ch'ojen Li, head of the League, says that the delegation has already contacted the FBSU, the FASU, and the students' Tiananmen Square Headquarters, and it will get in touch with other organizations in order to find the best methods to distribute the donations from Hong Kong.

In the morning of June 3, a military jeep kills two people, and another two are badly hurt.

135

Tanks obstructed in the suburbs of Beijing.

Students wounded in clashes with the military at the gate of Zhongnanhai showing their bloody shirts.

In the afternoon of June 2, Hou Derchien (right) and three other intellectuals come to the Square to start their hunger strikes.

The banner reads, "Students are the pioneers; they depend on the people."

The Hong Kong Citizens Democratic Movement League brings money and materials to Beijing.

June 2 Hunger Strike Declaration
By Liu Xiaobo, Zhou Tuo, Hou Derchien, and Gao Xin

Today we have decided to go on a hunger strike. Our purpose is to protest, appeal, and confess.

We are not looking for death, but for a real life.

In the face of the mounting pressure of military violence by the Li Peng government, which has lost its ability to reason, Chinese intellectuals must end our "osteomalacia," which we inherited from the ancestors of our ancestors over thousands of years. We have indulged ourselves more in talking than in doing. Now we are taking action to protest the martial law, to call for the birth of a new political culture, and to confess the mistakes we made in the past because of our "weak knees." We are all responsible for China's being left behind by the rest of the world.

This democratic movement, unprecedented in Chinese history, has been using legal, peaceful, and rational means in an attempt to achieve freedom, democracy, and human rights. However, the Li Peng government moved hundreds and thousands of troops to suppress the students and civilians, who did not have a single inch of iron. Therefore, our strike is no longer intended as a petition. Ours is a protest against the government's martial law. Although we prefer the peaceful ways of democratic progress to violence of any form, we are not afraid of violence. We will show through peaceful demonstrations how much potential strength lies in the people's support for democracy. We want to break the iron order that has been maintained by lies and bayonets. To employ troops and martial law in order to crack down on the peaceful petitioners was an absurd and stupid decision that has already become a stain on China's history. It resulted in great humiliation for the Communist Party, the government, and the People's Army, and it destroyed the achievements that we made during ten years of openness and reform.

Chinese history, which covers several thousand years, is filled with instances of pacifism replaced by violence. In recent times, hostility among people is still a problem in social relations. Since 1949, the slogan "Class struggle is the key link" has represented the extreme form of this traditional hostility and the violent overthrow of dynasties. The current martial law is also part of the political "class struggle" culture. The purpose of our fasting is to appeal to the people to cast off the hostility among us and to abandon the idea of "class struggle." We must learn that hatred can only lead to violence and dictatorship. Chinese democracy must be built on the basis of tolerance and cooperation. Democracy is a political form excluding enemies and hatred; it requires mutual respect, forgiveness, and cooperation in making its decisions after discussion and voting. Li Peng made serious mistakes in the office of premier; he should step down according to democratic procedures.

However, Li Peng should not be considered our enemy. When he is out of his office, he will enjoy the rights that a citizen does. He can, if he chooses, hold on to his wrong political ideas. We call upon every citizen from the government level to the grassroots to abandon the old political culture. We want the government to stop martial law immediately and resume dialogues between the students and the government in order to resolve the conflict.

The student demonstration has received support and understanding from the Chinese people in all walks of life. The exercise of martial law has in fact turned the movement into a nationwide democratic undertaking. But we have noticed that a lot of support came from people's dissatisfaction with the government and from their sympathy for the students. The people lack the concept of political responsibility. We therefore want to gradually raise their awareness of citizenship and help them give up their status as onlookers or sympathizers. Citizenship means, first, political equality for everyone. Everybody should know that his political rights are the same as those of the premier. Second, citizenship means not only justice and sympathy, but rational involvement in politics, that is, political obligation. It is not enough for the individual to express his sympathy and support. He should join in the building of democracy for China. A good political structure in a society comes from the participation of everybody living in it. Likewise, all the people share the responsibility for a bad political structure in their society. A citizen has the divine responsibility to take part in social politics. The Chinese people must know that in the democratic process of politics, everybody is first and foremost a citizen, then a student, teacher, worker, cadre, or officer.

For thousands of years, Chinese society has been circling from one emperor to another. We overthrew the old emperor only to establish the crown of another. History has proven that the replacement of an unpopular ruler by a popular ruler does not resolve China's political problems. What we need is not a perfect savior but a good democratic system. Therefore, we appeal for the establishment of independent organizations by the people at all levels so as to form a political force to work with the government in policy-making. Because at the center of democracy is this equilibrium, we would rather have ten contending devils than one omnipotent angel. We also appeal for a solid, workable system of discharging officials who make serious mistakes in office. We understand that it is not important who comes into power, but how he gets there. Non-democratic designations and dismissals can only lead to the concentration of power in the hands of a dictator.

During this movement, both the government and the students have made mistakes. The problem with the government was that it was controlled by the old "class struggle" theory and took a stand against the students. That theory led the conflict from bad to worse. The problem with the students was their lack of structure and thought. In the course of their fight for democracy, anti-democratic elements appeared in their words and deeds. Therefore, we appeal to the government and the students for calm examinations of the past few weeks. On the whole, we consider the government responsible for the severity of the whole situation. Demonstrations and hunger strikes were democratic ways for people to express their wills. They were consistent with the Constitution and should not be seen as "turmoil." The government ignored the citizens' basic rights guaranteed by the Constitution and wantonly determined that the student movement was "turmoil." As a result of a series of wrong policies issued by the government, the demonstration escalated again and again, and the conflict worsened. We may well say the "turmoil" was actually incited by the government; its consequences are no better than those of the Cultural Revolution. Because the

students and civilians held themselves back and because many of the important people from the society appealed very strongly for non-violence, large-scale bloodshed has been avoided so far. The government must admit and acknowledge these mistakes. We think it is not yet too late for the government to do so. The government should learn an important lesson from this democratic movement and listen to the people's voices. They should also get used to people's using their constitutional rights to express their wishes and govern the country through democratic procedures. The nation-wide democratic movement is teaching the government how to do these things.

The students' problem was in the confusion of the federation structure and the lack of efficiency and democratic procedures. They used non-democratic means to fight for democracy. They announced democracy as their theory, but they did not use it in coping with day-to-day routines. They lacked the spirit of cooperation, so their strength was wasted in conflict. Their decisions were temporary and inconsistent. The student leaders did not know how to manage money and materials. They were more emotional than rational and more involved in exercising their individual power than in practicing the democratic idea of equality.

For about a hundred years, the Chinese people's democratic movement focused mainly on ideological concepts and slogans. It engaged itself in discussing the basic ideas of democracy and its goals but seldom touched the actual operation of democracy or its procedures and methods. We think that democratic politics is realized by democratizing government operations, means, and procedures. Therefore, we appeal to the Chinese people to switch from empty talk of democracy at the level of enlightening to the solid study and practice of building a working democracy. We must begin this with every little job we are doing now. The students may want to start this examination with their demonstrators in the Square.

One of the big mistakes that the government made was its use of the term "a handful." We want to tell the world through fasting that this "handful" are not students but civilians who, driven by their political obligations as citizens, took part in the student democratic movement. What they did was reasonable and legal. They want to use their wit and energy to force the government to realize, acknowledge, and correct its mistakes in politics, in exercise of justice, and in personality cultivation. They wish the student independent organizations would gradually complete their own structures in the light of democracy and law.

We must acknowledge that to practice democracy in Chinese politics from the central government level is new to every Chinese citizen. Therefore, the people as well as the top leaders must start the lesson from the beginning. Mistakes cannot be avoided during the learning process. The key to success lies in the willingness to learn from our mistakes and correct them as soon as possible. In that way, we can turn mistakes into precious experience and master the democratic operation of our country.

Our basic tenets:

1) We have no enemies! Do not allow hatred and violence to poison our wit and hamper the progress of the democratization of China.
2) We need to reexamine the past. Everybody is responsible for the underdevelopment of this country.
3) We are, above all, citizens.
4) We are not looking for death, but for a real life.

The details of our hunger strike:

1) place: the Monument to the People's Heroes at Tiananmen Square.
2) time: seventy-two hours, from 4:00 P.M. June 2 to 4:00 P.M. June 5, 1989. (Note: Because Hou Derchien will be going to Hong Kong on a business appointment regarding the production of his records in six days, his hunger strike will end at 4:00 P.M. June 4)

The cartoon shows Deng playing bridge; his card says "The Chinese way of modernization."

139

3) regulations: except water, no food or drinks of nutritious liquid, such as those containing sugar, starch, protein, or fat, are allowed.
Names of hunger strikers:
Liu Xiaobo: Ph.D. in literature, lecturer in Chinese literature department, Beijing Normal University.

Zhou Tuo: former lecturer at the Sociology Research Institute of Beijing University, now director of General Planning and Development of SiTong Group, Inc.
Hou Derchien: well-known composer and song-writer.
Gao Xin: former chief editor of Beijing Normal Weekly, CCF member.

June 3, Saturday; June 4, Sunday
Massacre

The Xinhua news agency broadcasts the full text of a "mobilization order for action." Entitled "The Importance of Realizing the Nature of the Turmoil and the Inevitability of Martial Law," the eight-thousand character document was written on June 2 by Li Zhijian, director of propaganda of the Beijing Municipal Government and one of five members of a propaganda group under Li Peng. It is carried by newspapers, radio, and television, as an obvious order to mobilize in preparation for the massacre.

Surrounding armies force their way into Beijing, provoking incidents along the way to incite the people to fight. In the early morning of June 3, four tourist shuttle buses used to transport supplies are caught at Jiangoumen and Xidan and surrounded by civilians. Inside, machine guns, rifles, grenades, and gas masks are discovered, arousing great anger among those who are present. The weapons are put on display at Xinhuamen Gate and attract more than ten thousand people. During the day, plain-

On June 3, large groups of soldiers rush into Beijing.

clothes military personnel are discovered in town, probably familiarizing themselves with the city map, which they have been doing for several days. At noon, about twenty military people and armed policemen come out of the west gate of Zhongnanhai, all wearing steel helmets and carrying electric clubs. They close the streets of Xidanfu Youjie and Liubukou, separating the crowds of Xidan and Xinhuamen Gate. The armed police broadcast a warning for about twenty minutes while throwing twenty tear gas bombs and waving their clubs to scatter the crowds. A serious confrontation arises. Soon after, between two and three hundred military personnel dash out from Xinhuamen Gate. They strike whoever is in their way with long wooden sticks and electric clubs. Chaos occurs in front of Xinhuamen Gate, where the students of the University of Politics and Law have been holding a sit-in for half a month. At Xidan, the troops use rubber bullets to suppress the demonstrators; many are wounded. (Later, people pick up about forty bullets.) Around two, while tear gas is exploded at Xidan, nearly ten thousand troops rush out of the west gate of the People's Hall trying to block the intersection of Ximen Road and form a clo-

sure. However, civilians have jammed the north and south directions with two big buses. A crowd of about a hundred thousand people gathers there. The stand-off lasts between two and three hours. At 4:30 some students try to talk with the military, but without success. Suddenly rocks come flying towards the troops and confusion follows in which both soldiers and civilians are injured. The troops later withdraw into the Hall. Meanwhile more than a hundred thousand people gather on Changanjie Avenue, and the armed policemen and military police have withdrawn from Xinhuamen Gate and Xidan. The angry masses turn a jeep upside down at an intersection, smash a traffic police post and break all the windows of two tourists buses that were delivering weapons to the spot. . . . Since the morning of June 3, confrontations between troops and civilians have not stopped, and both sides are becoming more and more agitated. . . .

After six P.M., the radio and TV stations issue three emergency orders signaling the forthcoming violent suppression. At 6:30 the first emergency order is on the air from the municipal government and the headquarters of the martial law units. It warns

Thousands of citizens try to stop the troops.

everybody in the area to obey the martial law. "Should anyone ignore this advice and challenge authority, the martial law army, police, and armed police have the power to use whatever means necessary to force him to obey the order." The second order, broadcast at about 8:30 P.M., reiterates that the army can tolerate no more and will adopt all possible measures to remove the obstacles. At this time, there are several hundred thousand students, workers, and civilians in the Square. At ten P.M. the third order comes, warning people to stay inside their houses to avoid danger. But the number of people in the Square remains the same. The atmosphere is very tense. Later when some

A student displays one of many weapons found inside a captured tank.

foreign and Hong Kong news reporters recall the incident, they say that when the third order was broadcast, the first shots were fired at Huangzhidun, near the Xinhua News Agency, and one witness said that people fell down instantly. Shortly after eleven, gunfire started at Muxidi, near the residential areas of high-ranking officials.

The rounds of fire at ten and eleven P.M. indicate that more troops are moving into the city. Although no one knows for sure how many soldiers enter the urban area, the number is believed to be over ten thousand. They approach Tiananmen Square from all directions. At 12: 20 A.M. of June 4, the first armored car proceeds full speed along Changanjie Avenue from the west. The crowds in the street try to block it with human bodies, but the carrier will not slow down. The people barely escape the murderous vehicle. A second car comes following the same route. They destroy all obstacles in their path, apparently preparing the way for the military vehicles behind. One armored car that enters East Changanjie Avenue is stopped and held up at Jiegoumen Gate by the civilians. The people rush the car into the middle of the boulevard to block later armored cars. There are more than ten military personnel in the car, but it is knocked over by the next armored vehicle, and all the soldiers inside are thrown out. One is killed immediately and the rest are all injured.

The following are glimpses recounted by an eyewitness of the massacre.

The beginning of the massacre: At 12:57 A.M. on June 4, fires are evident and series of gunshots are heard from the Square in the distance, but it is difficult to tell whether they are tracer bullets or not. At 1:05 A.M., from Chongwenmen district, south of Tiananmen, tracer explosions are seen in the sky accompanied by gunshots. At 1:25 A.M. about six hundred soldiers in four or five columns march in the direction of the People's Hall from the south. They keep shooting into the sky; the distance narrows down to only a hundred meters between the panic stricken people and the army. At 1:40 A.M. these troops arrive at the Hall. By two o'clock fire and smoke come up everywhere along Changanjie Avenue.

The massacre: Beginning at two in the morning, the "army of people's sons and brothers"—the 27th army—have encircled the thousands of people who are too late to leave the square. At four, the "square cleaning" action starts. Showers of hollow-point bullets fly out of the gun barrels, screaming through the darkness of the night. The lights in the Square go on and off irregularly; crying, machine-gun roaring, shouting, tommy-gun firing, and wailing fill every corner of the place. The tanks' rumbles, the butchers' laughter and the victims' shouts of "Long live the people!" blend in a horrifying, deafening noise. A hush suddenly falls on the Square. Then the sirens of the Red Cross ambulances awaken the numbed senses of the survivors. How many youths were shot down in that short period, and

A student showing an electric club to people.

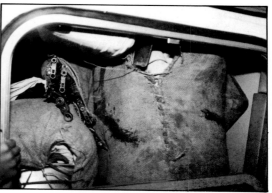

Weapons found in a shuttle bus.

A bloodied worker describing his beating by soldiers.

how much blood was shed in Tiananmen Square? Not even the survivors can tell the exact number. This marked another page in the history of the disasters suffered by the Chinese people. It is unthinkable that the "people's government" order the "people's army" to slaughter the people whose money supports them.

Burning corpses to destroy evidence: June 4, gunshots are everywhere; the capital of the republic is in the midst of an ongoing war. After daybreak, piles covered by canvas or students' tents are seen in the Square. A helicopter lands, its propellers blowing off a canvas and exposing the dead bodies to daylight. In spite of the all-night washing and cleaning, huge patches of blood can be seen here and there. . . . (For days after June 4 tanks are arrayed in the square while military people wash and clean the ground.

The armed police in Xidan district use electric clubs and tear gas to dispel the crowd.

A student holds a soldier's hand and tries to dissuade him from going to Tiananmen Square.

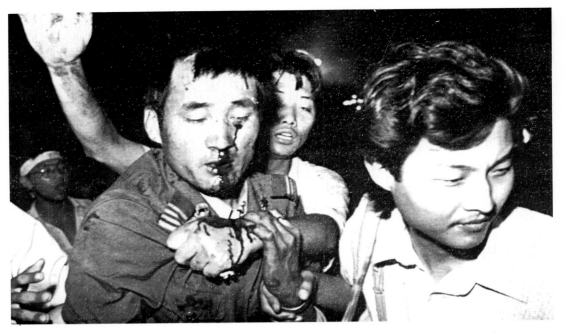

Tank crewman being helped by students after being beaten by citizens. His tank had crushed several people and was stopped by fire.

An armored car on fire.

They put up metal frames to burn the lifeless mass and then remove them from the spot by helicopters.)

Beijing falls in gunfire and smoke: The 27th army continues its task of "quelling the counter-revolutionaries." Wherever they go, there are gunshots. Among the "counter-revolutionary rioters" is a nine-year-old child who received nine bullet wounds. Another child of about three or four was

Citizens killed by troops.

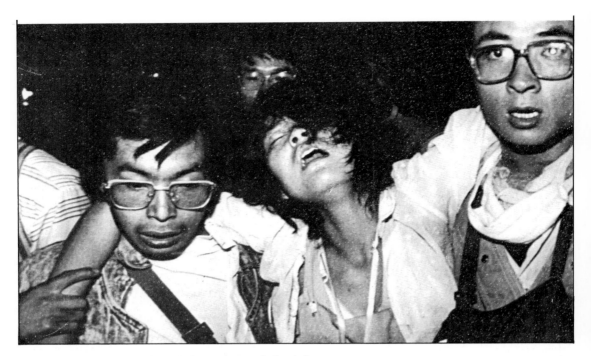

A wounded girl is carried by several other students to the hospital.

Tanks rolling into Tiananmen Square on Sunday morning.

shot seven times. One hospital tells reporters that the dead came to their mortuary ranging in age from thirteen to seventy. Some witness at Liubukou saw a soldier slaughter a three-year-old with his bayonet. . . . It is estimated that, among the people treated in the hospitals of Beijing, the death toll came to over twenty-six hundred. The injured filled all the rooms, and even the hallways were used as wards; surgeons had to operate on the wounded where they were. (Editor's note: the death count on June 5 was over five thousand and more than thirty thousand injured. On June 6, the death toll exceeded seven thousand. These figures did not include those who disappeared. It is possible that those who disappeared in the Square on the morning of June 4 have become dust and will never reappear.)

In the morning light, bicycles and the bodies of students are strewn everywhere in Tiananmen Square.

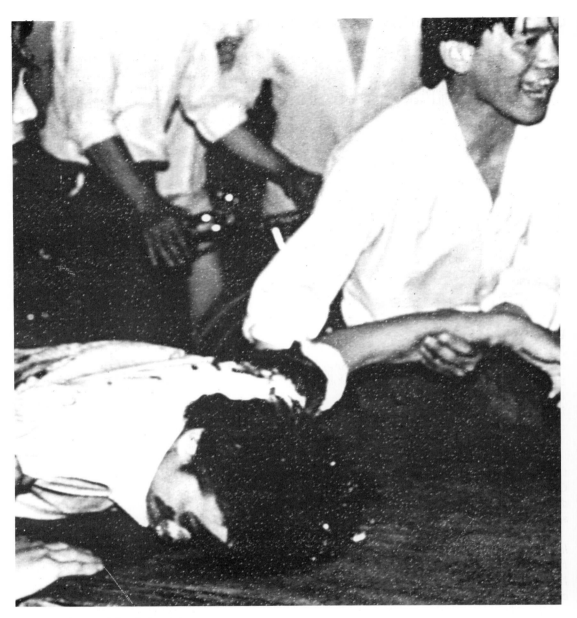

Rushing the wounded to the hospital.

Chai Ling's Narration of the Massacre

Chai Ling.

Editor's note: On the evening of June 10, Radio and Television of Hong Kong (RTHK) broadcast a recording of Chai Ling, a major student leader in Beijing. Chai Ling recalled the happenings of the night of the massacre in Tiananmen Square. This is an edited account of her narration.

It is now four o'clock in the afternoon of June the eighth, nineteen eighty-nine. My name is Chai Ling. I was the chief commander of the student headquarters in Tiananmen Square. I am still alive.

I think that I am best qualified to relate the happenings in the Square during the time between June 2 and June 4. I feel obliged to tell the truth to everybody here, and through you to every fellow citizen, every Chinese.

About ten o'clock on the night of June 2 came the first signal of the massacre: a police car ran over four innocent people. Three of them died. Then we found some soldiers unloading guns and army uniforms and distributing them to the students and civilians around them. We were very suspicious of their actions, so we collected those materials and forwarded them to the police. We have kept the receipts as evidence. The third signal arrived at 2:10 P.M. June 3 at Liubukou and Xinhuaman Gate when armed police attacked our students and civilians. The students had been standing on top of carts and crying out

through loudspeakers. They were shouting: "The People's police must love the people!" and "The People's police do not beat people." The students had hardly finished the words when one student got kicked in the belly by a policeman who climbed up the cart. The policeman yelled "Who the hell loves you!" and gave him another blow on the head. The young man fell down at once.

Let me explain our operation in the Square. I was the chief commander. We had set up a broadcasting station that mainly reported the news of the hunger strike. I was always there directing the students' actions in the Square. There were, of course, other people at the station, people like Li Lu, Feng Congde, etc. We constantly received emergency information about students and civilians being beaten and injured in different parts of the Square.

Things became worse and worse as the time dragged from eight, to nine, to ten o'clock. At least ten news reports about people being attacked by the military were received in that period of time. We held a news conference for the reporters on the site. Unfortunately there were very few foreign correspondents, probably because they had been confined to their hotels by the military. We were also told that their rooms had been searched. Only one or two foreign press personnel managed to enter the Square.

The headquarters issued a statement. We put forward one single slogan, which was, "Overthrow the Li Peng government."

At nine o'clock, all the students in Tiananmen Square stood up, raised their right hands, and pledged: "In order to push forward the democratic process of our motherland, to realize prosperity in our country, to avoid a handful of conspirators draining our great motherland, and to save the 1.1 billion Chinese from losing their lives in the white terror, I pledge to use my young life to defend Tiananmen and to defend the republic. My head may be cut off, the blood may flow, but Tiananmen Square must not be lost. I will fight until the last person falls."

At ten P.M. the Democratic University of the Square announced its opening. Zhang Boli, the vice–general commander, was appointed president. The university received warm congratulations from many individuals. Meanwhile, more and more emergency correspondence came to the headquarters. The situation was very tense. While cheers and applause rose like thunder from the site of the Goddess of Liberty where the university was announcing its existence, both east and west Changanjie Avenue witnessed bloodshed. The butchers of the 27th army used tanks, machine guns, and bayonets on anyone, even if he or she had only shouted a single slogan or had thrown one rock at them. They fired guns at them. All the dead bodies in the street had bullet wounds in the chest. Some of the wounded students came to the headquarters to inform us. Their chests, hands, and legs were covered in blood.

Since April the patriotic democratic movement, started as a student campaign, had developed into a nation-wide action supported by people from all walks of life in China. Our principal manner of demonstration has been peaceful petition. Quite a few workers, civilians, and students came to the headquarters and proposed to use violence against violence. Some of the male students were especially angry. We kept telling the crowds that ours was a peaceful demonstration and that the highest principle of peace is sacrifice.

Hand in hand and shoulder to shoulder, we moved slowly out of the tents towards the Monument to the People's Heroes and sat down around it. We were ready to receive the butchers' knives in peace. It was a war between love and hate, not between violence and battle forces. We felt that the patriotic democratic movement, which was based on the principles of peace, would fail if the students tried arming themselves with gas bottles and wooden clubs to resist the machine gunners and tank drivers, who had already lost their ability to reason.

The students sat quietly, waiting for the moment of sacrifice. The song "The Descendants of the Dragon" was played through the loudspeakers outside the headquarters tent. The students hummed with the music, tears in their eyes. We hugged each other and held hands. We knew that the moment had come for us to lay down our lives for the nation.

There was among us a little guy of fifteen. His name was Wang Li. He wrote his will. I do not remember the exact words of it, but I remember a story he told me about a tiny insect. He said every time he began to move his foot to crush it, the little creature would freeze. He was only fifteen, but he had started to ponder the meaning of death. Remember, People's Republic of China, the children who have died for you.

About two or three in the morning, we had to give up the headquarters and withdraw to the broadcasting station under the Monument. I walked around the monument to mobilize the students for the vigil. They sat in silence. They told me that they would sit firmly no matter what happened. They also promised not to use violence against their attackers.

I made a short speech. I said there is an ancient story in which about 1.1 billion ants lived on a hill. One day a fire broke out on the hill, and the only way to safety was to go down to the foot of the hill. To save themselves from the fire, they all clung to one another in a big ball, and tumbled down the hill. The ants that were on the surface of the ball were killed by the fire, but the majority were saved.

I told them that we were standing at the forefront of the nation, and we were all aware that only sacrifice could bring life back to this republic.

Holding hands together, the students sang "The Internationale" again and again. Finally the last four hunger strikers, Hou Derchien, Liu Xiaobo, Zhou Tuo, and Gao Xin could not hold their emotions any more. They said, "Children! No more sacrifice, please."

All of us were very tired. The four hunger strikers went to the military to try to negotiate. They found an officer who claimed to be responsible for the duties of the martial law headquarters and told him that the students would withdraw from the Square on the condition that the army guarantee the safety of the students. Meanwhile, the student leaders in the Square decided to withdraw after asking the opinions of the other students. However, right before we could pass the decision to our students, the troops broke their promise. Armed with helmets and machine guns, they charged onto the third level of the platform of the Monument. Our loudspeakers were crushed instantly. They were now firing at us on the people's monument, the Monument to the People's Heroes. The students came down the monument in tears. We were all crying in retreat.

People shouted at us, "Don't cry!" The students replied that we would return to the Square

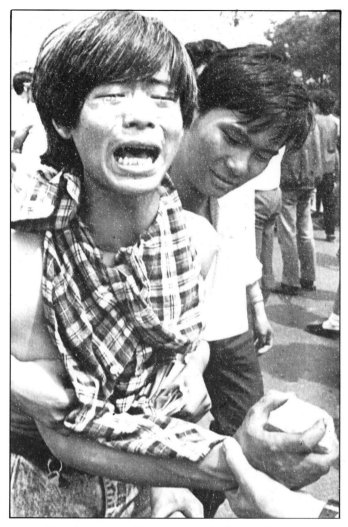

A tearful student is stopped from throwing a brick at a military car.

again, because it was our square. Later we learned that some of us still held illusions about this government and its troops. They thought the troops mainly wanted to force them to leave the Square. Fatigue had lulled them to sleep in their tents; tanks knocked their tents down and ground their bodies apart. Some estimated a death toll of two hundred; others said four thousand. I simply have no idea how many died in the massacre. But I know for sure that the members of the Workers' Independent Association all got killed. They were about twenty or thirty people.

It was said that while the students were discussing the issue of withdrawing from the Square or not, the armed forces poured gas over the tents, padded coats, and dead bodies of the students and then set them on fire. They planned to wash the Square later so that no trace of killing could be exposed to the public. The symbol of our democratic movement, the Goddess of Liberty, was likewise crushed.

Holding hands together, we walked around the Mao Tsetung Memorial Hall trying to find an exit on the west of the south side of the Square. We found about ten thousand soldiers in helmets sitting on the ground south of the Memorial Hall. The students shouted "dogs!" and "fascists!" at them. When we left toward the west, we saw column after column of troops running to gather in Tiananmen Square. The civilians shouted to them: "Dogs!" "Fascists!" "Beasts!" The soldiers did not even glance at us. They ran as fast as they could toward the center. When we passed by Liubukou, where one of the first bloody conflicts took place, the student leaders conscientiously walked in the front line. Debris, such as broken and burnt garbage bins, was everywhere. Between Liubukou and Changanjian Street, we saw vehicles damaged by fire, broken bricks and tiles left to remind us of the fierce fight the previous day, but no corpses. Later we learned that the troops collected the bodies that had fallen to the ground while they had forced their way forward. The bodies, some still alive, were dumped onto buses or tricycles, leaving no chance for the injured people to survive. They did their utmost to to hide their crimes.

We wanted to stand up, to demonstrate, and to return to the Square again, but all the people around tried to dissuade us. "Son," they said, "do you know they have loaded guns? Don't kill yourself for nothing." In the end, we decided to go to Xicheng, the west part of the city, by way of Xidan.

On the way to Xicheng, we saw a woman wailing. Her child had been killed. A little distance further, we saw four corpses, all civilians. Everyone we saw on our way to our schools had tears in his eyes.

One civilian said to us angrily, "Are we buying state bonds to allow them more funds to manufacture more bullets to kill our own children and innocent people?" More information came to us from different sources, such as fellow students and civilians. It boiled down to one single truth—the government troops were butchers and were slaughtering people. They had fired rocket guns at the residential houses along Changanjie Avenue. The victims were not only students and workers, but also old people and little kids. What crimes could the government accuse them of? They did not even shout one slogan! A friend of mine told me that he was among the crowds on Changanjie Avenue at about two A.M. They were trying to block the tanks. He saw a small girl waving her arms at the tanks that were coming in her direction. The tanks ran over her and ground her into pieces. My friend was holding two students by their arms. One bullet hit the student on the right in

the arm and he fell down. Shortly afterwards, another bullet hit the student on the left. My friend said, "I believe that death was only a tenth of an inch away from me."

We saw a woman looking for her son. She gave us his name and told us that he was alive yesterday. "Is he still there?" Many people were looking for relatives and friends. As we walked toward our schools, we found some office buildings hanging big posters supporting the "right" decisions of the Central Committee of the Communist Party. We got very angry, so some of us tore the slogan down and burned it.

All through the night the radio was broadcasting the message that "the military forces were moved to Beijing to quell a handful of rioters and to help the capital restore order." I think that I am in a position to determine whether we are rioters at all. Now, every Chinese who has a conscience, please put your hand on your heart and think about this: How can the young students be considered rioters when all they did was sit together on the platform of the monument. Do you call them rioters when they met the violence of the armed police without resistance? If those who shot at us are animals and beasts, those who sit in front of the cameras or on television screens are worse. They have degenerated to such a rotten base that they are not ashamed to tell lies. Just as we were leaving the Square, a tank ran after us with tear gas bombs knocking down several students, but it didn't care. It drove over the students' bodies. It crushed their legs and necks. Their bodies can never be put together again. Now, who are the rioters? You tell me!

We put on cotton masks because the tear gas was drying up our throats. We walked on and on, mourning our friends who had sacrificed their young lives. They are gone forever.

We finally got back to the Beijing University campus. The university had prepared accommodations for the students who came to Beijing to join us. But none of us wanted bed or food. We were very, very said. We are the survivors. Many of our friends died on the Square. They won't be coming back again. They will stay on Changanjie Avenue forever.

Our return to Beijing University marked the forced ending of the peaceful petition that started in the form of a hunger strike on May 13, 1989, and continued in the form of a sit-down through June 4, 1989. Later information came that, on the night of June 3, Li Peng issued three mandates: First, the army was authorized to shoot. Second, armored carriers were to move in at full speed, and Tiananmen Square was to be cleared before the dawn of June 4. Third, every leader and organizer of the movement was to be persecuted without mercy.

Friends, this is a chaotic government, but it is still moving troops to Beijing and it is still ruling the country. The Beijing massacre has just started. Gradually it will spread to the whole of China; it may have started in other parts of China already. Friends, let us have con-fidence in the future. The darkest period of the night comes right before the dawn. A real people's republic will be born in the awakening to the fascist suppression. This is a life-or-death moment for the Chinese nation. Arise, Chinese people. Arise, every citizen who has a conscience. The last victory surely belongs to you. It will not be long before the downfall comes to the government headed by Yang Shangkun, Li Peng, Wang Zheng, and Bo Yibo!

Down with fascism!
Down with military rulers!
Victory to the people!
Long live the Republic!

A student is manhandled trying to stop the soldiers.

What I Saw in Tiananmen Square: A University Student Bears Witness

Editor's note: This article was first published by *Wenhui Pao Daily* in Hong Kong and carried by several other newspapers in the following days.

I am twenty years old. I am a student from Qinghua University. All last night I sat on the steps underneath the Monument to the People's Heroes and witnessed the brutal suppression as the army fired on peaceful demonstrators.

Several of my friends are dead from gunfire. My clothes bear the blood they shed. As a survivor, I want to tell the peace-loving people of the world what I saw in Tiananmen Square.

To be honest, we received word yesterday afternoon that they had decided to resort to military force. We got an anonymous tip through a public telephone that the government was going to clear the Square by force very soon. A student leader, the one who got the news on the phone, spread the story among us and held an emergency meeting to discuss what we could do to lessen the conflict and avoid unnecessary bloodshed.

At that time, we had twenty-three submachine guns and a few incendiary bombs that we had taken from the army during a conflict two days earlier. In order to reaffirm the original purpose and spirit of the "non-violent push for democracy," the Autonomous Student Union decided at that meeting to return the weapons to the army. We spoke with soldiers under the huge portrait of Chairman Mao at the gate of Tiananmen, but only to be told by an officer that they did not have the authority to accept the weapons.

Seeing that there was no way to give the weapons back and that the situation was getting worse with every passing minute, some students started to break the guns and dismantle the bombs by hand. They emptied the gas from the bombs so that no one could see them to blame the students for slaughtering soldiers. That was about one A.M.

Then the Autonomous Student Union broadcast an announcement urging the students and civilians who were still in the Square to leave, because the situation had become very dangerous. About forty or fifty thousand students and

a hundred thousand other protestors refused to move. I was one of them.

When I recall what happened last night, it still terrifies me. None of us had had any experience like that before in our entire lives. Anyone who was there and claims not to have been afraid has to be lying. Just the same, most of us were fully prepared and convinced that if we died, we would be dying for democracy in China and for China's future. That feeling of mission inspired us constantly. And there were a few of us, of course, who did not believe the army men would ever fire on us.

At twelve o'clock, two armored carriers drove from each side of Qianmen and charged through the Square toward Changanjie Avenue. While the government loudspeakers broadcast an "Emergency Notice," hundreds of thousands of troops wearing helmets gathered on the perimeter of the Square and moved in a circle toward the center. On the roof of the History Museum, machine guns were glimpsed in the midnight darkness.

Those of us who stayed in the Square gathered under the Monument to the People's Heroes. I made a rough count; among the students, one third were women. Beijing students made up about thirty percent of the total; the majority were students from other parts of China.

At about four o'clock, just before dawn, all the lights on the Square suddenly went out. The order to clear the Square came again from the government loudspeakers. A deep chill went through me. The time had come. The time had come.

Hou Derchien and some of the other hunger strikers had managed to negotiate with the troops and agreed to a peaceful withdrawal of students from the Square, but as soon as the students started to leave—about 4:40 A.M.—red signal flares rose and exploded above us, and at the same time all the lights came back on. We saw then that the soldiers occupied the vast front part of the Square. The next moment, more troops—these were in camouflage uniforms— came running from near the east gate of the Great Hall of the People. They had submachine

The poster reads: "The people will win."

guns, helmets, and gas masks. At six o'clock on the day before, we had met with some officers of a regiment at the west gate of the Hall and were told by the commander that they were only a reinforcement. He promised us there would be no firing on the students. He also told us that the army meeting the students directly would probably be the Sichuan army. So we thought this might be the Sichuan army now, marching into the Square.

The first thing they did after they reached the front of the Monument was set up a dozen submachine guns. The gunners lay on their stomachs, directing their guns at the monument, where we were gathered. Immediately after this, a large group of military personnel and armed policemen broke into our sitting lines; they all carried electric clubs, rubber rods, and some other stuff we had never seen before. They beat us with the clubs and rods until they had cleared a path to the third level of the monument platform. I saw about forty or fifty students with their faces bleeding. Right at that moment, the troops waiting in the armored carriers came out to join the siege. Troop carriers and soldiers on foot moved around us to form a tight circle, leaving an exit near the Museum.

Meanwhile, the troops attacking the monument began to destroy our broadcast equipment, duplicating machines, and even the soft drinks we had saved. Then, using the clubs, they tried to drive us down the platform. None of us moved at first; we sang "The Internationale" and shouted "The People's army does not beat people." But we were finally driven down.

When the students from the third level had moved down to the ground, the submachine guns started firing. Some soldiers shot from a kneeling position, and their bullets flew over our heads. Some shot from a lying position; their bullets hit students in the chest and head. We regrouped and tried to move back up to the higher platforms of the Monument. The machine guns ceased firing, but the clubs and rods forced us back to ground level. As soon as we were off the Monument, the guns started to fire again.

At this moment, the "dare-to-die corps" of workers and others ran frantically toward the army with bottles and sticks. A few minutes before five o'clock, the Autonomous Student Union gave the order to leave the Square.

We headed to the Museum, where we thought we could escape through the exit we had seen a moment before. But we were wrong.

The armored carriers had sealed the opening. About thirty carriers pushed toward the crowd. Some students were knocked down and crushed. Even the flagpole in front of the Monument was toppled. The square was filled with a wild confusion of noise and movement. I have never seen my fellow students act so bravely as last night. Some of them tried to turn the carriers over to make an exit. When they were shot down, others replaced them. We finally turned one carrier over, leaving an opening through which I and the other three thousand students ran. By the time we reached the Museum, there were only one thousand of us.

We joined the crowd at the gate of the museum just as the crowd started to move north, away from the gunfire and toward the Tiananmen Gate. We had moved only a few yards when firing was heard from the trees to the north. We could not see anything but the flashes of guns. We turned and ran south, toward Qianman Gate.

I was crying as I ran. Those at the front of the crowd ran into a rain of bullets. A few yards further on, I found a lot of bodies lying on the ground. We couldn't help crying, running for our lives and crying. Finally we reached the gate but we came face to face with troops marching from the direction of Zhubaoshi. Instead of guns, they were armed with wooden clubs. They began to beat us as hard as they could. A huge crowd of people at Qianman Gate came to our aid, and a fierce riot broke out. With the help of our increased numbers, we broke out of the encirclement and turned toward Beijing Railway Station. The troops were still coming after us. By five o'clock in the morning, the firing in the square had died away. Later, a classmate I saw at the International Red Cross told me that those who were not too severely injured to run had gotten out of the Square before five. The shooting had lasted about thirty minutes.

I will never forget a student of Qinghua University, a native of Jiangsu Province. He was bleeding from several bad wounds, but he was still running with us. Then, probably because he had lost so much blood, he stumbled into my shoulder from behind. "Would you take my arm for a moment . . .?" he said in a faint voice. I was supporting an injured girl on each side, and before I could free my arms to help him, he fell to the ground. He was trampled by the fleeing crowd. . . . He must be dead now. Look, the blood stains on my shirt are his. Half his body was covered with blood when I last looked at him.

And I will remember always how students ran to rescue the wounded and carried the dead home at the risk of their own lives. Some women students took their shirts off to make bandages for the injured.

After we reached the railroad station, three of us went back to the Square. It was six o'clock. The area around Qianman Gate was packed. I followed the crowd, trying to see as much as possible of the Square, but we were stopped near the Mao Tsetung Memorial Hall by walls of soldiers and armored carriers. I climbed a tree. From there I could see soldiers collecting dead bodies, dumping each into a plastic bag, piling them together, and then covering the piles with large canvases.

Back on the ground, I ran into a student I had some classes with. He had gotten out of the Square later than I did. The death toll was enormous, he said, but the soldiers wouldn't allow anyone to help the dying, not even the ambulance crews from the International Red Cross. At the First Aid Center set up by the Red Cross, we learned that the wounded who were lucky enough to be brought there had arrived in tricycle cabs. The doctors told us that an ambulance trying to pick up wounded students was fired on by troops and caught fire. I talked to more students who got out of the Square late. They told me that when they left the place near dawn, a lot of injured students were lying on the ground.

Around 7:20 I went back to the Square again. This time I talked to some older people. They told me that the sidewalks of the Square had been loaded with dead bodies lying side by side. They saw soldiers hanging canvases to try to hide the scene. Later, they said, more carriers came to the Square. The injured were placed in the carriers and taken away.

Around 7:30 A.M. the soldiers in the Square suddenly fired gas at us, and then charged in our direction. I ran to the station again. On the way I passed several groups of students. They were all crying.

The Autonomous Student Union asked us to take the students from other cities to the station and put them on the train. I took some of them, only to be informed by the railroad authority *that the railways were all cut. We left the station not knowing where to go. Crowds quickly gathered around us; some people offered to give the students shelter in their homes. Everyone was very sad; some were still weeping. The people of Beijing are a great people. They are very, very special.*

How many died? I do not know. But the day will come when the Chinese people find out.

Am I pessimistic? No, I am not. I am not, because the movement has demonstrated the Chinese people's will and their spirit, which are the hope of China. Some of my friends are dead; others are bleeding. I am a fortunate survivor. I know now how to live. I will always remember those who died in the cause of a democratic China. And I am aware now that we are not alone. The good people of the world understand us and support us in our struggle.

June 5, Monday
The Government Announces Victory over the Counter-Revolutionary Turmoil

Gunfire is still heard from time to time; tanks and military vehicles are seen patrolling the city. More people are wounded, and the hospitals are depleting their blood supply. Since the bloody crackdown in Beijing, the capital has collapsed into confusion and horror. Between early morning of June 4 and midnight of June 5, shots are heard in many places, but there is no way to determine the cause of the gunfire. Information from various channels says that there is a major gun battle at Nanwan Airport. People also hear cannons firing. The sound of gunshots from Nanwan Airport does not die down until the evening of June 5. Streets on the outskirts of the city are deserted, but the downtown is in chaos. Civilians keep coming to the streets to watch what the troops are doing from a distance. A number of damaged armored carriers and civilian vehicles burn in the streets near Tiananmen Square. Dark smoke rises from the burning mess. The ruins of trucks and tanks are seen everywhere. About a hundred tanks are lined up at the entrances of the Square in battle positions. Clashes between troops and unarmed civilians are constant, often ending in shooting. Lots of people fall, wounded or dead. Hospitals are packed with the injured, and mortuaries fill with dead bodies. Most of the hospitals have used up the last of the blood from the blood banks. Although volunteers come to hospi-

tals to donate blood, many victims still bleed to death.

Radio and television announce that the counter-revolutionary turmoil has been quelled. On June 5, Central TV announces "A Joint Message to the Whole Nation from the Central Committee of the CCP and the State Council" and a "congratulation letter" to the martial law units from the PLA's General Political Department, the Headquarters of the General Staff, and the General Logistics Department. Both letters claim "success in quelling a shocking counter-revolutionary turmoil" and claim that the turmoil was perpetrated by the remnants of the Gang of Four and those who stubbornly hold on to a capitalist liberal stand. The TV announcers dress in black and speak in a very low tone. The Central People's Radio also announces the two letters.

It is learned that the army opened fire at the mass demonstration in Chengdu at dawn on June 4, killing about three hundred people, as it was estimated early that morning. Some reporters say that it started in a confrontation between students and armed police, but the official newspapers describe the appearance of the army as a necessary measure to quell rioters who have begun looting. Although the crackdown in Chengdu happened almost at the same time as the massacre in Tiananmen Square, it is not known to the outside until June 6.

About 5:20 A.M. a motorcade of four cars, fourteen minibuses and vans, nineteen military jeeps, two police cars, and a couple of tanks in the rear slowly drives out of Zhongnanhai and then turns northeast along Changanjie Avenue, causing a lot of speculation among observers.

After the massacre, many rumors float around Beijing, but none of them can be confirmed. One major story is that Deng Xiaoping is hospitalized because of cancer. Another says that the 38th army is fighting against the 27th army at Nanwan Airport. It is said that Zhao Ziyang is hiding in the diplomatic district of Beijing and that the

Tanks patrol the streets after the massacre.

Confrontation between the army and the crowd. Whenever the crowd gathers, the army opens fire.

Transporting the wounded to the hospital.

troops of the General Staff have been disarmed by the 27th army. There is also news that a large-scale crackdown occurred in Sichuan Province in which two thousand people died and sixty thousand were wounded. Other rumors say that the 38th army rebelled first, that Fang Lizhi has taken refuge in the American Embassy, and that student leaders Wuer Kaixi and Wang Dan are dead. . . .

Memorial services are held around the world to mourn those who died in the Beijing crackdown.

Tianjing, Shanghai, Nanjing, Hangzhou, Wuhan, Xian, Lanzhou, Changsha, Guangzhou, Changchun, Harbin, and other big cities see huge crowds, mostly students, pouring into the streets to mourn the people who died in Beijing. They hold memorial services to protest the government. Similar

After the massacre, tanks patrol the streets, and wrecked buses are everywhere.

protests appear in middle-sized and small cities, too.

About a hundred thousand angry and sorrowful civilians in Hong Kong and Macao pay respects to the dead in Tiananmen Square. Since June 3 when a memorial service location was designated near the entrance of the Xinhua News Agency, Hong Kong branch, people have thronged to the place bringing flowers and wreaths that form a pile more than three hundred yards long. On June 4, one hundred thousand people hold a vigil at Happy Valley to mourn the Chinese victims in Beijing. They decide to start a campaign in which everybody writes one letter to China to tell the Chinese people about truth. A similar public memorial service site is set up in front of the Macao branch of Xinhua News Agency. About ten thousand people go there to mourn. All the newspapers in

Hong Kong and Macao carry extensive coverage of the memorial services.

The Central Committee of the National Party in Taiwan expresses its keen concern over the Beijing Massacre and mourns those who died. Memorial rallies are held spontaneously in Taipei, Taichung, and Kaohsiung. Many student unions donate

President Bush meets with a Chinese student, showing his concern for the pro-democracy movement in China.

Six hundred Chinese students demonstrate in Bonn to protest the massacre.

money to aid those wounded during the massacre.

In almost all the cities and towns where there are overseas Chinese, public memorial services are held voluntarily, especially in Canada, America, Britain, and France. In Tokyo, about twenty thousand Chinese demonstrate and shout slogans opposing Deng Xiaoping and Li Peng.

The military crackdown shocked the United States, Britain, Canada, France, Switzerland, Holland, Japan, and Australia. The United States suspends all relations with China. Holland appeals to the Common Market countries for a joint response. Australia has cancelled her warship's visit to Shanghai. The Japanese Communist Party has issued a statement condemning the Chinese Communist violence. The Soviet Communists express regret over the crackdown. The Yugoslavian prime minister postpones his trip to China. The official Yugoslavian news agency refers to the bloody massacre of Beijing as the "destruction of illusions, and a symbolic sacrifice for the sake of ideals. But these ideals have been crushed by tanks and machine guns."

A Joint Message to the Nation from the Central Committee of the CCP and the State Council

Communist Party members, and all the people of China:

The capital of China, Beijing, is in a critical state. A handful of people with ulterior motives have been instigating turmoil for over a month. Since the early morning of June 3, this restlessness has become a shocking counter-revolutionary riot.

These few rioters incited people who did not know the truth to commit criminal acts. They blocked the martial troops that were on their way to guard the urban areas of Beijing and Tiananmen Square. They smashed and set fire to more than one hundred armed trucks and public transportation vehicles. They also insulted, beat, and kidnapped cadres, soldiers, and armed police. They grabbed guns, ammunition, and other military supplies. These people tried to break into the Party's headquarters, People's Hall, the Central Broadcasting and Television building,

Li Peng announces "A Letter to the Chinese People" after the crackdown.

Public Security offices, and other important offices in Beijing. They looted shops and burned police posts. In addition, they killed several dozen PLA soldiers and armed policemen. They even hung the dead soldiers' bodies from the rails of a highway bridge. The purpose of the turmoil is to negate the Party's leadership and the socialist system, in order to overthrow the People's Republic of China. They openly shouted, "Take up arms and overthrow the government!" They also shouted "Kill all forty-seven million Communist members in China." The organizers of the turmoil are a few bad elements who, for a long time, have persisted in bourgeois liberalism and political conspiracy. They worked with foreign enemy forces and provided illegal organizations with confidential information about the Party and government. The rioters who did the burning, beating, and killing were those who had criminal records and had not been properly rehabilitated. Among the rioters we found political rogues, remnants of the Gang of Four, and other scoundrels. In short, they were a group of counter-revolutionaries who fiercely hated the Communist Party and the socialist system.

As everybody knows, for over a month the government has demonstrated the greatest patience in coping with the turmoil, which involved mostly people who did not know the truth. However, this handful took the government's restraint as weakness that they could take advantage of. They escalated their activities, finally leading to the counter-revolutionary riot. Confronted with such a violent situation, the People's Liberation Army had no choice but to take resolute measures to quell the riot. In order not to hurt innocent people, the martial law troops repeatedly announced emergency notices beginning the afternoon of June 3 to try to persuade the people and students to leave the Square. The army did their best to avoid bloodshed. Nevertheless, some rioters paid no attention to the army's advice. They attacked the troops in a frenzy. As one would expect under the circumstances, some injuries occurred. Most of them were PLA soldiers and armed police. We

did not want this to happen. On the other hand, if we had not taken this measure, we could not have quelled the riot. We may need to shed more blood in the future, or the People's Republic government, which the revolutionary martyrs built with their lives and their blood, will be overthrown. All the achievements of socialist construction and the ten-year reform program will be destroyed in one night. The whole country will be covered in reactionary white terror. And so, we were absolutely right in quelling the riot. It was the will of the people in the capital and of the whole nation.

By relying on the officers and soldiers of the PLA martial law units, on police and armed policemen who fought bravely, and on the support of the majority of students and civilians, we have taken the first step toward victory. We must, however, be keenly aware that the counter-revolutionary riot is not over yet. These few will not recognize their failure, and they will go on making trouble and wait to launch a comeback. Comrades and citizens, we must alert you to this continuing complicated situation. Let us unite and stand firm in the struggle to defend the revolution, to protect the fruits of construction and reform. If they dare to make more trouble, we will wipe them out. We are sure that the final victory will belong to us because we are guided by Marxism and backed up by the powerful people's democratic dictatorship. We have tens of millions of Communist Party members and several million PLA men who are faithful to the Party and people. The majority of the workers, peasants, intellectuals, and Chinese democratic party members are supporting us.

All Communist Party members, people, and patriotic individuals must respond to the Party and government's call. You should be able to distinguish right from wrong, to take the whole situation into consideration, and to act immediately to resist the rioters. Do not do anything that will please your enemy but antagonize your friends. You must have faith in the Party and government's ability to quell the riot. Party members must act as role models for the rest of *the nation. Workers must stay on production lines to produce more to ensure the supply. They should also help to protect the social order. Party organizations at all levels must reinforce positive persuasion and political ideological work. Be patient with the students and the majority of the people. Listen to no rumors, and make no contacts with organizations.*

We shall fight to create a peaceful and stable order for our country. Let us unite and continue the success of socialist construction and the task of further reform.

June 5, 1989
The Central Committee of the
Chinese Communist Party
The State Council

June 6, Tuesday
Embassies Evacuate Foreign Nationals from China

The situation in Beijing intensifies rapidly; embassies begin to evacuate their nationals from China. Information from different sources often conflicts because the martial law armies control the centers of propaganda, broadcasting, and communications. But

Terror spreads in Beijing; the foreign embassies evacuate their people.

an examination of the various reports shows that the antagonistic feelings between the army and the Beijing people are still strong. The situation is grave. The martial law troops are active in the city, and gunshots are frequently heard. It is said that a few armed policemen and some machine gunners attacked the 27th army, which had been engaged in the bloody crackdown.

Shanghai citizens set fire to a train that killed six people who tried to stop it, June 7, Shanghai.

June 7, Wednesday

A well-supplied army marches near the foreign embassy district. A window of the American Embassy is broken by bullets. After reporting the emergency to their home government, many embassies decide to evacuate their families and nationals from China. American President Bush expresses his concern over the situation in China. He says he will temporarily suspend Sino-American relations and that he is looking for ways to get in touch with the Chinese leaders, but he is not recalling the ambassador. Many embassies have begun to make flight arrangements for staff and their families to leave the country. CAAC is not yet closed down; the airport is packed with passengers waiting to get on board.

For days memorial meetings are held across the country from Harbin in the north to Guangzhou in the south, and from Shanghai in the east to Lanzhou in the west.

Shanghai, Wuhan, and Chengdu's responses to the crackdown are especially strong. Tourists arriving in Hong Kong from mainland China tell reporters that Shanghai, Wuhan, and Chengdu are holding big demonstrations to protest the crackdown in Beijing. Students from Fudan University in Shanghai have been out on the streets for several days. In Wuhan, half a million protestors hold a vigil on the Nanjing Yangtze River bridge, blocking north- and south-bound railway traffic for days. Chengdu has yet to recover from the aftermath of the crackdown since June 4. In Shanghai, a train kills about thirty people who are lying on the tracks in protest; angry civilians set the train on fire, and it burns until the next morning. In Chengdu, on June 8, civilians would set fire to People's Market and two movie theaters.

The Government Announces a Student Death Toll of Twenty-Three and a Most-Wanted List of the Pro-Democratic Elements

On June 7, a news conference to announce the casualties is given by Yuan Mu, the spokesman of the State Council, and Zhang Gong, commander of the martial law units in Beijing. Yuan Mu says an incomplete investigation shows that during the suppression of the counter-revolutionary turmoil, about seven thousand people were wounded; among them, five thousand PLA soldiers and two thousand civilians. He says that approximately three hundred people were killed, but only twenty-three of them were students. He later confirms the student death toll, saying it is a reliable figure.

Dead bodies fill the hospitals.

After killing four citizens, this soldier was burned to death and hung on a bus.

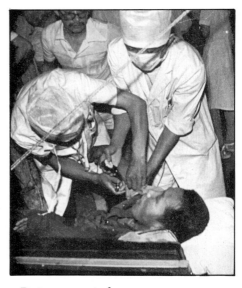

Doctors rescue a tank crewman.

Beijing Municipal Government declares that the Federation of Beijing Autonomous Student Unions (FBSU) and the Federation of Beijing Autonomous Workers Unions are illegal organizations and orders the leaders of the two organizations to surrender themselves to the police. If they do not give themselves up, the police will arrest them. At the same time, several hot-line telephones are set up for people to report to the police any information about the "counter-revolutionaries at large." The government warns the members of the two organizations that they must return to their factories or schools immediately and report their presence to the unit authorities. Observers consider this a signal of forthcoming large-scale arrests.

On June 8 tanks of the 27th division move away from Tiananmen Square.

June 8, Thursday
Li Peng Praises the Martial Law Army

On the CCTV evening news of June 8, Li Peng appears for the first time after the military crackdown in a reception for the martial law army to praise their victory. The news is provided by the martial law army headquarters, and it is divided into three parts. Li Peng and his colleagues—Wang Zheng, the vice president of the state, and Lu Gan, general secretary of the State Council—appear separately in three different scenes. News analysts consider the show an indication that Li Peng has gained the upper hand. Nevertheless, the situation is still confusing.

The 39th army replaces the 27th and the 38th in continuing to enforce martial law in Beijing. The 27th army left the capital under cover of darkness. The 38th army, which is in opposition to the 27th, also disappears from near the Military Museum. On the morning of June 9, Beijing people encounter

the new soldiers of the 39th army. They are friendly and smiling.

It is reported that a high-ranking official in charge of propaganda in Beijing criticizes the *Ming Pao News*, *Wenhui Pao News*, and *Dagong Pao News* of Hong Kong, accusing the three newspapers of "being used by a

Li Peng appears on television on June 8.

169

handful of counter-revolutionaries to incite turmoil." The official also attacks Li Zisong, director of *Wenhui Pao News* and Zha Liangyong, chairman of the Board of Directors of Ming Pao Group, both well-known in the Hong Kong newspaper business. He calls Mr. Zha Liangyong an "old-line anti-communist element." It is said that soon after the crackdown, the Li-Yang clique will further "clean" institutions that are formed mainly by Chinese intellectuals and arrest large numbers of intellectuals who are in China at the moment and, when conditions become convenient for the government, square accounts with those who are overseas. At present, *Ming Pao, Wenhui Pao,* and *Dagong Pao* are all banned by the Chinese customs house.

None of the student leaders who organized the demonstrations in Beijing has been seen in public since the crackdown. No one knows whether they are alive or not. On June 8, Chai Ling, the general commander in Tiananmen Square, records her account of the happenings before and during the massacre.

A contrast between the slogan and the reality. The slogan says, "Build a clean and beautiful city."

Deng Xiaoping shows up on June 9 and calls for "firm continuation" of his policy.

June 9, Friday
Deng Xiaoping Finally Appears in Public to Show His Power

Since Deng Xiaoping met Soviet leader Gorbachev on May 16, he has been devising strategies behind the scenes. He reappears on the evening news on June 9 receiving all the high-level officers of the martial law troops. Accompanying him are Li Peng, Yang Shangkun, Li Xiannian, Qiao Shi, Yao Yiling, Peng Zheng, Bo Yibo, Wan Li, and Wang Zheng. Zhao Ziyang and Hu Qili are not in the group. The TV news is short, but it shows the Communist hard-liners' unified position in sending troops to suppress the democratic movement. Deng Xiaoping praises the martial law army and proposes to stand in silence to mourn the military personnel who lost their lives in the crackdown. Deng condemns the pro-democratic elements, saying that "their purpose is to destroy the Communist Party and the socialist system, and to overthrow the People's Republic of China in order to establish a capitalist government." He speaks of the army as worthy of the names of "the people's army" and "the country's iron and steel wall." He says it stood the test in the quelling of the turmoil and proved its qualifications. He makes no comment on the student and civilian victims who died in the massacre. Before the reception ends, he pronounces that "all the lines, policies, and directions of the Party since the Third Conference of the Thirteenth Congress of the CCP are correct. One center, two basic focuses, persistence in the four cardinal principles, and an open-door policy are all correct. We must be firm in practicing them . . ."